LADY GAGA

Recent Titles in Greenwood Biographies

LADY GAGA

A Biography

Paula Johanson

GREENWOOD BIOGRAPHIES

 GREENWOOD

AN IMPRINT OF ABC-CLIO, LLC
Santa Barbara, California • Denver, Colorado • Oxford, England

Library of Congress Cataloging-in-Publication Data

Johanson, Paula.
  Lady Gaga : a biography / Paula Johanson.
    p. cm. — (Greenwood biographies)
  Includes bibliographical references and index.
  ISBN 978-1-4408-0109-9 (hardcopy : alk. paper) — ISBN 978-1-4408-0110-5
(ebook) 1. Lady Gaga. 2. Singers—United States—Biography. I. Title.
  ML420.L185J64   2012
  782.42164092—dc23   2011043427

ISBN: 978-1-4408-0109-9
EISBN: 978-1-4408-0110-5

16 15 14 13 12   1 2 3 4 5

This book is also available on the World Wide Web as an eBook.
Visit www.abc-clio.com for details.

Greenwood
An Imprint of ABC-CLIO, LLC

ABC-CLIO, LLC
130 Cremona Drive, P.O. Box 1911
Santa Barbara, California 93116-1911

This book is printed on acid-free paper ∞

Manufactured in the United States of America

For Marlena, the fashionista who says to wear jewel tones

CONTENTS

SERIES FOREWORD

In response to school and library needs, ABC-CLIO publishes this distinguished series of full-length biographies specifically for student use. Prepared by field experts and professionals, these engaging biographies are tailored for students who need challenging yet accessible biographies. Ideal for school assignments and student research, the length, format, and subject areas are designed to meet educators' requirements and students' interests.

ABC-CLIO offers an extensive selection of biographies spanning all curriculum-related subject areas including social studies, the sciences, literature and the arts, history and politics, and popular culture, covering public figures and famous personalities from all time periods and backgrounds, both historic and contemporary, who have made an impact on American and/or world culture. The subjects of these biographies were chosen based on comprehensive feedback from librarians and educators. Consideration was given to both curriculum relevance and inherent interest. Readers will find a wide array of subject choices from fascinating entertainers like Miley Cyrus and Lady Gaga to inspiring leaders like John F. Kennedy and Nelson Mandela, from the greatest athletes of our time like Michael Jordan and Lance Armstrong to the most amazing success stories of our day like J.K. Rowling and Oprah.

While the emphasis is on fact, not glorification, the books are meant to be fun to read. Each volume provides in-depth information about the subject's life from birth through childhood, the teen years, and adulthood. A thorough account relates family background and education, traces personal and professional influences, and explores struggles, accomplishments, and contributions. A timeline highlights the most significant life events against a historical perspective. Bibliographies supplement the reference value of each volume.

INTRODUCTION

Welcome to Lady Gaga—pop singing superstar and fashion icon. She writes her own songs, plays in her band, and is a promotional machine. She is a media darling for writers with a deadline, editors with pages to fill, and especially for photographers. There is always something to say about Gaga. She's always promoting a new release, or speaking at a rally. There's always some new costume to photograph, or some outrageous or inflammatory comment to quote.

The most trivial of changes in her kaleidoscope of costumes evokes questions. Otherwise sensible journalists have been known to ask Gaga when her hair bow accessory will be back. "The hair bow never left. She just goes to sleep sometimes," says a tweet—a note that Gaga sent out on Twitter in 2011. "She's very serious and methodic about her reinventions."[1]

Gaga is serious and methodical herself about her own reinventions. Among all the studied oddities in her repertoire, Gaga has played at more than one piano elevated several feet above the stage. The most recent of these elevated keyboards is based on a sculpture made by Gaga's younger sister, now an art student. The sculpture is made of coiled wire in the shape of a high-heeled shoe with the top of the heel some eight feet above the floor. An art piano like that could be isolating for the performer. But when it's time to get down, Gaga holds out her hands to the players in her band, and that connection brings her down safely.

Gaga is connected to everybody. Forget about the games "Six Degrees of Separation" or "Five Degrees of Kevin Bacon," because her connections are direct. In 2011, Gaga told shock radio host Howard Stern that her first piano teacher was also a stripper. Stern was fascinated to learn that the woman had danced at Scores, one of his favorite New York clubs. The story got Stern wondering if back in the day, he had ever had a lap dance from Gaga's piano teacher.

Of all the people to give a testimonial to Gaga, Sir Elton John is an unexpected ally. They became friends when they performed together at the Grammy Awards in 2010. "What I like about Gaga the most is that she's amazingly polite and respectful to everyone around her. . . . But the greatest thing about her is that she manages to let everyone think they know everything about her but no one knows anything," said Sir Elton. When the animated feature film *Gnomeo and Juliet* needed a duet, Elton John and Gaga recorded a song together. Their friendship has continued. "She's a phenomenal star—definitely someone who will be taking on the old sods like me, McCartney and Rod Stewart doing big tours for years to come. Pure genius."[2] He has considerable admiration for her marketing and promotion skills, as well as her performing talent.

Even Oprah Winfrey has come to love Gaga. "I fell in love with Lady Gaga during a moment on my show when someone stood up and said, 'Thank you for being who you are because you being who you are has made me proud to be myself,'" Oprah told a writer for *Vogue* magazine. "Listen: I teared up over that. And so did she. It gave me goose bumps. When *you* being who you are makes somebody else proud to be his or herself? I don't think you can do any better than that. She's not just eccentric. She makes a lot of people accept their own differences— and other people's. It's real for her."[3]

Everyone has something to say about Lady Gaga. The controversial documentary maker Michael Moore wrote on his website in 2009 that he didn't know this Lady Gaga, but he found her performance on *Saturday Night Live* to be fascinating. During a flight that October, he listened to Gaga's music on his personal music player.[4] He made a point of uploading a video to his own YouTube channel of her statements at the Portland, Maine, rally. Months later, Moore also posted Bill Quigley's article on "Why Wikileaks Is Good for Democracy," commenting on "Private Bradley Manning, who, according to the Associated Press, was able to defeat 'Pentagon security systems using little more than a Lady Gaga CD and a portable computer memory stick.'"[5] Moore's political analysis now includes Lady Gaga.

Now, that is a bit of a stretch. Gaga may have gotten into the WikiLeaks story "like Pontius Pilate got into the Creed" (an expression that Bertolt Brecht used in his play *The Caucasian Chalk Circle*) but she's still in it. And, as always, she's still being talked about as if she has managed to get away with something. "In fashion, you know you have succeeded when there is an element of upset," Gaga commented on her blog *Amen Fashion*. "In pop, you know you have succeeded when there is an element of crime."[6]

NOTES

1. Lady Gaga. *Twitter*. Posted May 22, 2011. Retrieved May 24, 2011. http://twitter.com/#!/ladygaga.

2. "Sir Elton: 'Gaga Will Have Long Career.'" *Daily Star*. Posted February 4, 2010. Retrieved April 2, 2011. http://www.dailystar.co.uk/posts/view/175194/Sir-Elton-Gaga-will-have-long-career-/.

3. Van Meter, Jonathan. "Oprah Goes Gaga." *Vogue*. July 2010, p. 120.

4. Moore, Michael. "Pilots on Food Stamps." *Michaelmoore.com*. Posted October 11, 2009. Retrieved March 26, 2011. http://www.michaelmoore.com/words/mike-friends-blog/mikes-blog-1-pilots-food-stamps.

5. Quigley, Bill. "Open Mike: Why Wikileaks Is Good for Democracy." *Michaelmoore.com*. Posted November 30, 2011. Retrieved March 26, 2011. http://www.michaelmoore.com/words/mike-friends-blog/why-wikileaks-is-good.

6. Lady Gaga. *Amen Fashion*. Posted July 2011. Retrieved August 10, 2011. http://amenfashion.tumblr.com/.

TIMELINE: EVENTS IN
THE LIFE OF LADY GAGA

March 28, 1986	Born Stefani Joanne Angelina Germanotta.
March 28, 2002	Permitted by parents to begin dating.
2002	Independent release of unnamed demo recording.
June 2003	Graduates from Convent of the Sacred Heart High School New York City.
September 2003	Enters Tisch School of the Arts at New York University.
2005	Independent release of extended-play recordings *Words* and *Red and Blue*.
May 24, 2005	Becomes member of MySpace.com.
September 2005	Signed to Island Def Jam Records.
January 8, 2006	Dropped by Island Def Jam Records.
June 2006	Scouted by Wendy Starland at New Songwriters Showcase.
2007	Signed to Interscope Records.
Spring 2008	Just Dance promo tour.
May 15, 2008	Starts ladygaga video channel at YouTube.
2008	Opening act for New Kids on the Block: Live Tour.

August 29, 2008	Releases album *The Fame*.
2009	Opening act for Pussycat Dolls' Doll Domination tour.
	The Fame Ball tour.
May 11, 2009	Starts ladygagavevo video channel at YouTube.
September 13, 2009	Performs "Paparazzi" at MTV Video Music Awards.
Fall 2009	The Fame Kills tour with Kanye West scheduled and cancelled.
Fall 2009	The Monster Ball tour.
2010–2011	The Monster Ball tour 2.0.
September 24, 2010	Death of paternal grandfather Giuseppe Germanotta.
February 11, 2011	Releases single "Born This Way."
April 20, 2011	"Weird Al" Yankovic releases parody recording "I Perform This Way."
May 23, 2011	Releases album *Born This Way*.
Fall 2011	The Born This Way Ball tour begins.

Chapter 1

A HIGH-ENERGY PERFORMER

The most famous superstar musical performer in the world these days, hands down, is Lady Gaga. The secret of her fame is no single event or a simple thing. It's not just how she sings and dances in concerts and videos. It's more than just how she dresses, which ranges from provocative to outrageous. And while her statements about equal rights for gays and believing in yourself definitely contribute to her notoriety, that isn't all that keeps her in the news. Lady Gaga owes her colossal success to combining all her considerable talents with the single-minded purpose of putting herself out in the public eye.

"No one knows how to get press attention better than Lady Gaga. We're talking about her right now," video journalist Anna Kasparian pointed out, when discussing Gaga's appearance at the Emmy Awards in 2011. "Everyone's talking about her."[1]

There's one more element as well that keeps her at the center of attention: she tries to give all that attention and adoration back to her fans. When she is the focus of a crowd of 40,000 people in an arena, Lady Gaga does her level best not only to give good value to her fans but to admire them as well. She wrote on one of her album covers about the "sharable valuing that is fame." For Gaga, her fame is not something that she keeps for herself. She makes it a point to share it with her fans.

WELCOME TO THE FUTURE

Popular culture guru Andy Warhol is famously quoted as saying that in the future, everyone would be famous for 15 minutes. The world has now arrived at Warhol's future, but Gaga's fame is lasting more than just a few moments. "In little over a year Lady Gaga has rocketed from struggling as a performer in New York to the glamorous life of a world-wide phenomenon," wrote one analyst. "From her outrageous outfits to elaborate live shows and out-spoken politics, her life is one grand performance."[2]

"Released at the end of the Decade of Celebrity, the Warholian message of Lady Gaga's *The Fame*—nowadays, we're all superstars—was timely and almost profound," wrote Graeme Thomson for *The Observer*. He went on to say, "Railing against the 'noise of mediocrity,' the . . . New Yorker, otherwise known as Stefani Joanne Angelina Germanotta, not only unleashed a series of fantastically hook-laden singles, she also dressed exactly the way a pop star should, complete with fire-breathing breasts. Without her blend of Streisand's imperiousness, Freddie Mercury's showmanship, Bette Midler's bathhouse cabaret and the young Madonna's sass, chutzpah and ambition, the future would be looking considerably duller."[3]

Journalist Joe Zee likened Gaga to Aphrodite. "Just as the goddess of love arose from the ocean a fully formed dewy beauty, . . . so has Lady Gaga, our value-added new pop star, seemed to arrive from nowhere, not exactly dewy, but, to use one of her favorite words, shiny, to give a depressed, industrialized globe supercatchy, highly danceable songs plus a more-than-we-bargained-for arsenal of outrageous costumes; fixating, idea-laden videos; claims to performance art; and gay rights activism."[4] By May 2011, Lady Gaga had sold more than 69 million singles and 22 million albums worldwide. As of June 2011, she has sold almost 7.2 million albums in the United States alone.

The subject of thousands of articles in print and electronic media, Gaga has been called "bizarre, a drag queen, fierce, a hermaphrodite, a gay man trapped in a woman's body, a self-parody, outlandish, hard-core, trashy, genius, futuristic, grotesque. All that's missing, so far, has been for the Catholic Church to weigh in," declared a writer for *Vanity Fair*. "She is, without question, the world's biggest pop star, and says Jimmy Iovine, who heads her record label, Interscope, 'We haven't had one of these phenomenons since Eminem. I'm talking about impacting haircuts, everything.'"[5]

"She reminds me of all the great pop women who have preceded her and, at the same time, none of them," said MTV chairman and CEO Judy McGrath, as quoted in *Vanity Fair*. "Pop tends to mow through people quickly, but Gaga is still at the beginning of where she is going."[6]

KEY ELEMENTS

The intense stage presence of Lady Gaga has been called exhaustive, as well as exhaustively entertaining. The audience doesn't just sit back and relax at her shows. "She's a hell of a singer, who flaunted the power of her big, dark voice in an extended version of 'Teeth,'" enthused reporter Rupert Everett-Green, "reveling in the song's florid gospel implications seconds after singing such lines as 'I just want your sex.' She belted out lyrics while romping down a catwalk, and kept singing even after diving into the crowd during 'Alejandro.'"[7]

When Gaga performed during her Monster Ball tour, a troupe of dancers and musicians accompanied her onstage. The stage was filled with a set designed to evoke New York City, or a version both idealized and gritty. Fire escapes were lit with neon. There was even a miniature subway car. Under the hood of a turquoise-green car, something like one formerly driven by one of her boyfriends, there was a keyboard. At one point in the show, Gaga smeared herself with fake blood. At another point, she dueled with a giant puppet monster.

"Her songs were mostly about sex, fame and ambition, but whenever Gaga spoke, as she did frequently and at length, she gave personal sermons about the power of positive thinking and of being who you are. 'One day, you will have a stage on which to sing and dance and shine before all who bullied you,' she told her 20,000 fans, as if speaking to herself in a mirror," wrote Everett-Green about her Toronto concert. "She mutilated Barbie dolls and lay flat on the stage to speak to Jesus. She preached the virtues of love and unity, then delivered incantations of rage against all those who ever slighted her dreams and abilities."

As her career has grown, Gaga has shown "an instinct for teasing media and fans alike with her chart-topping disco songs, over-the-top fashion fantasies, theatrical innovations complete with gender-bending sexual branding," wrote Denis Armstrong for Sun Media. "But in the end, it's mostly fodder for the tabloids when compared to the imaginative brilliance of Gaga's extraordinary live performance."[8]

"[U]nlike many other young stars, Gaga is not just a cute singer with nice pipes at the front of a slick, hyperproduced packaging machine," pointed out a writer for *ELLE* magazine. "She writes her own songs, plays her own keyboard, and—this is harder than it sounds—doesn't lip-synch her live concerts."[9] There are few times that Gaga has ever lip-synched a performance. For example, once on tour in Australia she woke up with her voice almost gone, and lip-synched a song during a television interview. There were complaints from fans, and apologies from Gaga, and her voice recovered.

"Unlike anyone else who ever sang while sitting at a piano—from Carole King to Tori Amos—Gaga has pianos that are actually part of her attire," commented journalist Lisa Robinson. "When she performed at the Museum of Contemporary Art in L.A. her piano was designed by Damien Hirst."[10] In just a couple of fast-paced years, Gaga has changed from being a student at New York University (NYU) writing essays about Damien Hirst to a world-famous performer collaborating with that celebrated artist.

The butterflies Hirst painted on that particular blue grand piano were somewhat tamer than the bubble piano that was designed to match Gaga's bubble dress. The bubble piano was an upright piano made from clear Plexiglass, filled with clear and silvered plastic bubbles. Lighted from inside, it shone onstage. For a while, it was Gaga's favorite toy. Another piano that traveled with her on the Monster Ball tour was a baby grand piano, made so that flames could flicker from the top.

"Whether she is playing a burning piano or one hoisted 30 feet in the air, Lady Gaga's performances (and outfits!) are out of this world," wrote one biographer with enthusiasm. "She also has the musical chops to keep her fans coming back for more."[11]

Lady Gaga at the Museum of Contemporary Art's 30th anniversary gala in Los Angeles on November 14, 2009. (AP Photo/Dan Steinberg)

WORKING ON THE ROAD

In every place she stayed on the Monster Ball tour, Gaga and her staff set up a portable studio from where she could work, usually backstage at the concert location. There were posters of the Sex Pistols and AC/DC, a large laptop computer, fan art, journals for handwriting notes, and photos of the Beatles and Bob Dylan. "I'll often stop in the middle of a quick-change backstage, I'll stop and look at the *Haus of Gaga* and say, Remember this! Write it down! And that's why we have those journals,"[12] Gaga explained to Ben Mulroney during an interview. Sometimes, inspiration strikes her in her dreams. "I'll wake up and sing something into my BlackBerry, call Fernando to come to my room and give it to them and they'll work with it."

Her schedule is exhausting, with evening performances set after busy days of interviews, photo shoots, and travel by jet between Los Angeles and New York or internationally. Sometimes a performance ends early— early by her and her manager's standards is before midnight. If so, Gaga often heads to a studio for a couple of hours and re-records the opening moments of a song currently being released as a single. She takes several sessions to record a series of openings, each highlighting the call letters of a different radio station. After several days, there's a special recording for every radio station in America. The local disc jockeys have no excuse not to play her songs. "Welcome to my life," Gaga said in an interview with *Rolling Stone*. "They can't say I didn't work for it."[13]

DANCE TILL YOUR FEET BLEED

While filming the "LoveGame" video, Gaga and her dancers were dancing on a cement floor. She wore a sky-high pair of shoes, designed by Christian Louboutin. The challenging choreography kept her on the move, and the shoes made deep cuts on her toes.

Eventually, after a long day in front of the cameras, Gaga took a moment during a brief pause in filming. She limped over to Laurieann Gibson, the creative director, saying that her feet were hurting. "You told me you wanted to be a superstar," was the reply from her choreographer. "You dance till they say cut."[14] Gaga went back to work for the last few shots, till the video was done.

DOING IT RIGHT

Is Lady Gaga primarily a singer, or a songwriter? Or is she a performance artist? "I call what I do art-pop, cuz I'm like a painter," she said on an *eTalk* prime-time special, broadcast on May 21, 2011. "When I'm making music it's like a wall." She sees each instrument, each part of a song, laid out like paint applied to a wall making a grand mural. She puts each part where she wants it, to make the best effect. When arranging songs for performance, she extends the process and incorporates the set design and her costume into the wall of creation.

Some critics might say that Lady Gaga is a performance diva, but Ben Mulroney disagrees. When hosting a special for *eTalk*, he observed Gaga during their interviews. Watching her concerts, he saw some of the backstage interactions. To him, Gaga is not a diva but a collaborator. He saw her checking in with her team time and again. He calls her one of a kind, but not above her fans.

It's not unusual that the influence of many other performers can be seen in Lady Gaga's songs and concerts. "All artists are influenced by those who came before them," wrote Robert Spuhler. He recommends the following recipe "to hatch your own Gaga: Two shots of Madonna . . . One shot of Ziggy Stardust . . . A splash of Gwen Stefani . . . Garnish with the Gobbledy Gooker."[15] Any performer who can be compared in one breath to David Bowie and in the next to a turkey mascot performing at the World Wrestling Foundation has clearly managed to develop a wide assortment of talents.

PREPARED APPEARANCE

Is Gaga truly beautiful? Who can tell? "In truth, Gaga's attractive, slightly off-kilter features—ethnic nose, prominent front teeth—seem almost infinitely mutable," wrote Brian Hiatt for *Rolling Stone*. "One day she looks like Debbie Harry, the next, Donatella Versace. But up close, she's always softer, prettier and younger-looking than her ultra-stylized photos might suggest."[16]

The look of Lady Gaga is no accident. From clothing to hair, makeup, and accessories, the way she looks keeps changing all the time, and always on purpose. "In Gaga's world," wrote one commentator, "where every swoosh of eyeliner, every wisp of hair, and every adhesive rhinestone is a thought-out gesture, there is no time for casual, no space for carefree, and no such thing as careless."[17] Whenever she sings at a festival or concert, the movements she and her backup dancers make are choreographed, even (especially!) the awkward moves that look clumsy. The music is scored and prepared and produced to be repeatable on cue.

"There is nothing on Lady Gaga's stage that she hasn't thought about," observed her biographer Lizzy Goodman. "Everything from the pattern on her dancer's fluorescent Hammer pants to the font on the *Haus of Gaga* sign to the individual light-up crystals on her 'disco stick,' she has either designed herself or consulted on. The entire stage has to reflect the aesthetic she's going for that night and her image as a whole."[18]

"I'm not supposed to be appreciated now," Gaga said to *eTalk* host Ben Mulroney on a prime-time special: *Lady Gaga—Born This Way*. "You'll appreciate me twenty years from now."

CRAFTED GENDER

Something important that Gaga learned from drag queens is the creation of onstage performances as a female entertainer. Drag queens transcend gender to create an onstage persona. Their feminine performances are social constructs, creations of clothing, accessories, makeup, and most of all behavior and voice. "Lady Gaga is explicit in her insistence that, since feminine sexuality is a social construct, anyone, even a man who's willing to buck gender norms, can wield it."[19]

Onstage, Gaga is acting out her role as carefully as any drag queen or female impersonator creating a tribute to a singer such as Cher or Barbara Streisand. It doesn't matter that this particular performer actually is a young woman. For each performance, her body is being artfully crafted into the illusion that she wants to present. When she is onstage, she doesn't look like a short, plump folksinger who is pretty in a way that looks healthy and rather ordinary. In platform heels, her shortness isn't apparent even though she is moving with dancers a head taller than she is.

"For Lady Gaga, genitalia are just another accessory," commented the author of a biography about the singer. "Maybe she has girl parts, maybe she has boy parts, but as long as you're talking about what kind of parts she has, she wins. In the end, everything about Lady Gaga, including her gender, is second to her fame."[20]

"People who have gone to her shows report that she comes across as both a huge, *sui generis* star and a vulnerable, even ordinary, everywoman. It's her ability to smooth out apparent contradictions—between the oppressive and the liberating, the cutting-edge and the awkward, the dazzling and the ordinary—that, I imagine, has a lot to do with Gaga's sky-high cultural capital at the moment," said philosophy professor Nancy Bauer. The Bauer interview appeared online, in a moderated blog run by editors of the *Encyclopedia Britannica*.

In an article she wrote for the *New York Times*, Bauer suggested that Gaga has a talent for "seeming to erase a potential contradiction between sexing oneself up to the max and being a powerful woman." One example of this ability that seems obvious to Bauer is the way that Gaga outfitted herself in nothing but carefully placed police tape in the "Telephone" video. It's common for people to compare Gaga with Madonna, partly because the Material Girl also had a talent for shock tactics and campy appeal, as well as a knack for getting mainstream culture to come along with her for a ride. "Lady Gaga strikes her fans as a liberating force: she seems to be able to transform what people ordinarily find oppressive into an opportunity for self-expression," said Bauer. "You might say that she's a specialist in the art of rack focus: she knows how to get a viewer to look at very familiar things in new and sometimes surprising ways."[21]

"That's how I originally became who I am. In New York I would play the piano and wig out in my underwear," Gaga said in front of *eTalk*'s cameras in 2009. On their prime-time special broadcast in 2011, she spoke of how people watching her perform in clubs would realize that she was confident in her music, and she was also confident enough to display herself in her underwear. "You can be a smart woman, you can own your sexuality, and you can be great."

BODY MAINTENANCE

The bodies of celebrities don't just happen to be beautiful, or strong, or limber. Even the people who start their performing careers at the peak of their health, vigor, and youth need to do work to maintain this condition. It takes a great deal of maintenance to keep a body limber and strong enough for dancing onstage, and slim enough to photograph well. For Gaga, that maintenance includes dieting, exercise, and health consultations.

Diet is an important element of Gaga's preparations. On at least two occasions since she was 18, Gaga has dieted in an effort to lose weight. As a person who is just over five feet tall, gaining or losing even as little as five pounds can make a difference to both her appearance and how her clothing fits.

It's been hard for her to change her diet though, as she finds junk food very tempting. Cream-filled cakes had special appeal for her in her late teens, and so did cans of potato chips. At that time, if junk food was available, she was likely to snack on it. "The pressure on her to [lose weight] was very high," according to her first producer's associate, Wendy Starland. "Her father bought her a membership at the Reebok Sports Club on the Upper West Side."[22] Regular visits to the gym helped Stefani (now known as Lady Gaga) lose 15 pounds.

Working out in sports clubs, gyms, and yoga studios is still part of Gaga's ongoing plan for success. Whether she is at her home base in

Lady Gaga steps off her private jet upon arrival at Sydney Airport, Sydney, Australia, July 9, 2011. (AP Photo/Dean Lewins, Pool)

New York, or on tour, workouts help her maintain health and strength. While on tour in 2011, Gaga brought along a couple of exercise machines and some sensible sneakers to make workouts easier.

When visiting a gym or studio, she doesn't make a habit of wearing leisure clothing such as sweatpants or sports leotards. This is because the paparazzi has taken to photographing her in idle moments or en route from one place to another. These casual photographs began appearing in the press during her first tour in the United Kingdom. Since that tour, Gaga has made an effort never to be seen in public dressed in sloppy clothes. She has a fear of being photographed like some celebrities have been seen, taking out their own garbage while wearing cutoff jeans and flip-flop sandals. Instead, Gaga has been photographed doing yoga sessions in black haute couture clothing and spike-heeled, knee-high studded boots.

HEALTH CRISIS

The life of a rock star on tour is exhausting. For Gaga, there is little or no time to party. After a performance, there's little time to wind down and relax. "I still smoke a lot of pot when I write music," Gaga admitted to Anderson Cooper in a television interview. "So I'm not gonna, like, sugar coat it for '60 Minutes' that I'm some, like, sober human being, 'cause I'm not."[23]

While opening for the Pussycat Dolls in 2009, Gaga suffered from exhaustion and strain during the tour in Japan. Visits to doctors and even hospitals showed mostly that she was overtired and dehydrated. After a vitamin shot and intravenous fluids, she'd try to get a night's sleep and a morning's rest before the next performance. There were similar spells during her Fame Ball and Monster Ball tours, because she led a similarly overactive schedule. Finally, doctors began doing further tests to see how her life of perpetual travel and little sleep was affecting her health. One of the tests was for lupus.

The reason for that test was because Gaga has an aunt who died at age 19, before Gaga was born. Diagnosed with systemic lupus erythematosus, her aunt Joanne Germanotta might not have died if modern treatments had been available. Lupus is an autoimmune disorder that can affect many parts of the body, including blood vessels, joints, and internal organs such as the heart, lungs, and kidneys. One of the names that doctors use among themselves for lupus is "The Great Imitator" because the symptoms are so vague, variable, and vast. It's easy for a doctor to confuse lupus at first with another kind of arthritis or rheumatic disease. With diagnosis and medication, the condition can be improved.

Tests showed that Gaga has inherited the genetic predisposition to develop lupus but probably does not have the actual condition yet. Her health is being monitored in case she develops lupus in the future. No one study has been able to throw light on exactly what causes this immune system problem. Good nutrition, physical activity, and reduced stress are usually recommended to promote immune system health.

ON HER PLAYER

The small personal music player that Gaga listens to carries a lot of music. At least part of the reason she listens to music in a personal music player is for the illusion of privacy. Anyone wearing headphones or earbuds has a private listening experience. The outside world is shut out, even if only a little. Since Gaga rarely takes a full day off, she needs to rest while traveling from one appointment to another. Her music player is always with her, like her BlackBerry smart phone.

It's understandable that to unwind, she doesn't make a habit of listening to her own work. But her listening choices might surprise fans who are more familiar with her pop music sound than with her past as a teenage performer. Her favorites include several varieties of heavy metal music, both older recordings and new material.

"What's on my iPod right now? I'm listening to a lot of AC/DC," she told a private television station in Malaysia while visiting the country during her Monster Ball tour in 2011. Her favorite bands include Motley Crüe, Led Zeppelin, and Queen. She quipped, "I like boys with long hair."[24]

This taste for heavy metal music isn't an inconsistency for Gaga, even though her own sound is a much softer, pop style of music. She listens to the music that reminds her of her young adulthood, when she was 18 or 19 years old, growing up as a performer in New York clubs. It's the music that she sang and danced to at that time, in a burlesque style punctuated with flaming cans of hair spray. That's when she met Lüc Carl, a bartender and musician who broke her heart and to whom she keeps returning as her career grows and changes.

TELLS

Poker players have a word—"tells"—for the unguarded moments when a person communicates something that he or she is trying to hide. Is someone bluffing or confident? In that unguarded moment, there's a giveaway gesture or expression, and a careful observer can find out. Even when a person tries to have a poker face, like Gaga wrote about in her song "Poker Face," there are times when feelings break through and are shown.

Journalists look for "tells" when they're interviewing celebrities. "In every *Rolling Stone* story, I looked for the moment when the artists drop their guard and reveal their true self," wrote journalist Neil Strauss. He found a moment like that in his interview with Lady Gaga. "Sometimes it's something dramatic like them getting arrested or wasted; other times it's some thing small, like a moment of insecurity or a childhood wound surfacing."[25] For him, that moment in their interview had Lady

Gaga wiping away tears. It was a very humanizing moment for the pop superstar who sometimes presents a robotic appearance.

"I like humanizing people. Like, say the Lady Gaga situation, everyone sees her as this narcissistic, crazy outfit-wearing cartoon character who creates this persona for everybody, but how can I break through to the real person inside? And I like that challenge," said Strauss when discussing his book of celebrity interviews. "I like finding that person and then sharing that person, so people can understand that person better. Whether they like them or don't like them, this is who they are."[26] In his interview with Lady Gaga, Strauss quoted her as saying that if she broke her leg in an accident, she wouldn't be seen by her fans wearing a cast. She would preserve the appearance she has worked to present.

"One thing I noticed is that people who are at the top and felt they deserved it, as much hubris as that is, often stayed there longer than those who got to the top and had doubts," commented Strauss. "One has to have some sense of deservedness and worthiness once one gets success."[27]

WHAT MONEY BUYS

"I really don't give a f**k about money at all," said Gaga to shock-radio host Howard Stern in 2011 when he tried to get the singer to talk about the gross income she's earned from her album sales and tours. The difference between gross and net income was something they weren't discussing. But personal wealth hasn't really motivated Gaga's climb to success. She still lives in a tiny Brooklyn apartment, though a bit bigger than where she lived after dropping out of NYU. Her wealth has bought only three real practical things: heart surgery and a car for her dad, and a house near Martha's Vineyard. Most of the rest of her personal earnings has been re-invested in accessories needed to promote the next tour. "The Monster Ball was really expensive and the next show will be really expensive and I will pay for it," she said of her next tour, planned for 2012.[28]

A REAL TROUPER

Little problems onstage may be frustrating, but Gaga doesn't let them stop a performance. There will certainly be a reckoning of what happened. If a problem was someone's fault, that someone might end up no longer working with Gaga after the show. For example, when a person had problems with the turntable onstage during Gaga's first performance at Lollapalooza, the problems brought an end to her time working with that person. But during a performance, if a microphone fails, for example, she takes another one and keeps right on singing.

While on the Monster Ball tour in Houston in April 2011, Gaga slipped off her piano and had a nasty fall. "The show must go on. That's the mantra in the entertainment business, right?" quipped reporter Paul Cantor. "If you're Lady Gaga, hell yeah it is."[29]

With one foot on the keyboard of her flaming piano, Gaga stepped down onto the piano bench stool. At once, the bench flipped outward. She fell, knees first on the wooden bench, before tumbling to land on her back between it and the keyboard. The stiletto heels on her knee-high boots pointed skyward. But as she was landing, she brought the microphone to her face. She kept singing the next line of "You and I" from her upcoming album *Born This Way*.

"Did she weep? No. She didn't even miss a beat, singing right on through the topple,"[30] reported an Internet media news site. The song was followed by a quick scenery change. Gaga came back onstage in seconds, wearing a different costume instead of her black bikini, an outfit that covered more skin. "You will never see me lip-sync," she screamed. "You will never see some rich bitch limping through a set."[31]

NOTES

1. Kasparian, Anna, and Cenk Uygur. "Lady Gaga In Egg, On Pot." *The Young Turks*. Posted February 14, 2011. Retrieved March 13, 2011. http://www.youtube.com/watch?v=35XEiJBpyzM&feature=fvst.

2. Herbert, Emily. *Lady Gaga behind the Fame*. New York: Overlook Press, 2010, promotional statement.

3. Thomson, Graeme. "Lady Gaga: The Future of Pop." *The Observer*. Posted November 29, 2009. Retrieved April 20, 2011. http://www.guardian.co.uk/music/2009/nov/29/lady-gaga-interview.

4. Zee, Joe. "Lady Gaga—An Exclusive Interview with ELLE's January Cover Girl." *ELLE*. Posted December 2, 2009. Retrieved April 29, 2011. http://www.elle.com/Pop-Culture/Cover-Shoots/Lady-Gaga.

5. Robinson, Lisa. "Lady Gaga's Cultural Revolution." *Vanity Fair.* September 2010, p. 280. http://ladygaga.wikia.com/wiki/Vanity_Fair_ (magazine).

6. Ibid.

7. Everett-Green, Rupert. "Lurid, Bitter, Swaggering, Maternal— and Oddly Real." *The Globe and Mail.* March 5, 2011. Globe Arts, p. R2.

8. Armstrong, Denis. "Concert Review: Lady Gaga Scotiabank Place, Ottawa—March 7, 2011." *Jam.* Posted March 8, 2011. Retrieved March 13, 2011. http://jam.canoe.ca/Music/Artists/L/Lady_GaGa/ ConcertReviews/2011/03/08/17532381.html.

9. Zee, "Lady Gaga."

10. Robinson, "Lady Gaga's Cultural Revolution," p. 280.

11. Parvis, Sarah. *Lady Gaga.* Kansas City, MO: Downtown Book-works/Andrews McMeel Publishing, 2010, cover flap.

12. Lady Gaga. "The Young Turks." *YouTube.* Posted February 14, 2011. Retrieved March 20, 2011. http://www.youtube.com/watch?v=3 5XEiJBpyzM&feature=fvst.

13. Hiatt, Brian. "Lady Gaga: New York Doll." *Rolling Stone.* Posted June 11, 2009. Retrieved April 15, 2011. http://www.rollingstone.com/ music/news/lady-gaga-new-york-doll-20090611.

14. "Lady Gaga Danced Until Feet Bled." *Daily Star Sunday.* Posted April 9, 2011. Retrieved April 9, 2011. http://www.dailystar.co.uk/ posts/view/185434/Lady-Gaga-danced-until-feet-bled/.

15. Spuhler, Robert. "How to Make a . . . Lady Gaga." *AM NewYork.* Posted February 21, 2011. Retrieved February 21, 2011. http://www. amny.com/urbanite-1.812039/how-to-make-a-lady-gaga-1.2703839.

16. Hiatt, "Lady Gaga."

17. Goodman, Lizzy. "In Search of the Disco Stick." *Lady Gaga: Critical Mass Fashion.* New York: St. Martin's Press. 2010, p. 115.

18. Ibid., p. 133.

19. Bauer, Nancy. "Lady Power." *Opinionator New York Times.* Posted June 20, 2010. Retrieved April 18, 2011. http://opinionator. blogs.nytimes.com/2010/06/20/lady-power/.

20. Goodman, "In Search of the Disco Stick," p. 115.

21. Levy, Michael. "Is Lady Gaga a Feminist? 5 Questions for Philosopher Nancy Bauer." *Encyclopedia Britannica.* Posted July 26, 2010.

Retrieved April 9, 2011. http://www.britannica.com/blogs/2010/07/is-lady-gaga-a-feminist-5-questions-for-philosopher-nancy-bauer/.

22. Wendy Starland, quoted by Callahan, Maureen. *Poker Face: The Rise and Rise of Lady Gaga.* New York: Hyperion/HarperCollins, 2010, p. 39.

23. Lady Gaga. "The Young Turks."

24. LadyGagaBeforeM. "Lady Gaga Interview 8TV Quickie Malaysia." *8TV Quickie.* Posted February 10, 2011. Retrieved March 24, 2011. http://wn.com/8TV_Quickie.

25. Strauss, Neil. "Interviews Gone Wild." *Rolling Stone.* April 14, 2011, p. 14.

26. Conner, Shawn. "Interview with Neil Strauss." *Guttersnipe.* Retrieved May 5, 2011. http://www.guttersnipenews.com/features/neil-strauss/.

27. Brown, Molly. "Neil Strauss' Everyone Loves You When You're Dead." *Kirkus Reviews.* Posted March 15, 2011. Retrieved May 5, 2011. http://www.kirkusreviews.com/blog/question-and-answer/neil-strauss-everyone-loves-you-when-youre-dead/#continue_reading_post.

28. Kaufman, Gil. "Lady Gaga Dishes on Sex, Drugs, Born This Way on Stern." *MTV.* Posted July 18, 2011. Retrieved July 20, 2011. http://www.mtv.com/news/articles/1667402/lady-gaga-howard-stern-born-this-way.jhtml.

29. Cantor, Paul. "Watch Lady Gaga Fall On Stage." *Complex Girls.* Posted April 12, 2011. Retrieved April 19, 2011. http://www.complex.com/girls/2011/04/watch-lady-gaga-fall-on-stage.

30. Ibid.

31. Hlavaty, Craig. "Friday Night: Lady Gaga At Toyota Center." *Houston Press Blogs.* Posted April 11, 2011. Retrieved April 18, 2011. http://blogs.houstonpress.com/rocks/2011/04/lady_gaga_toyota_center.php.

Chapter 2

PERSONAL BACKGROUND

"Since I was a little girl, I used to say to myself everyday 'My life is music, my life is art,'" Gaga was filmed saying on *eTalk*'s prime-time special *Lady Gaga—Born This Way*. "And it wasn't true, but I woke up and said it every day," she admitted in a video clip on June 21, 2009, shown at the Much Music Video Awards ceremony in Toronto. "And one day, I woke up and it was true. My life is art."

Gaga takes pride in integrating her performance into every aspect of her life. When she goes out to a meeting, it's as Lady Gaga, not as an anonymous woman. Even when she relaxes on the beach, it's in a metallic bikini top or with her cell phone nearby so she can send a quick photo and note through social media to her fans. But there was a time before her life became art, when Gaga was a little girl called Stefani.

When interviewed by tabloids and journalists, Gaga offers details about her youth and childhood that are colorful and interesting. Some of these details are different from the memories of her friends and classmates. Some of the details seem to be made up, to create the past she wants for the character that she has become. But one thing is consistent and constant in Gaga's stories of what it was like growing up as

Stefani, and that is the secure knowledge that she had the support of her loving family.

BORN IN THE USA

When Lady Gaga made her first appearance, she didn't have flamboyance and a stage name. She was born Stefani Joanne Angelina Germanotta on March 28, 1986, in Yonkers, New York. Her parents were Joseph and Cynthia Germanotta, Italian Americans who wanted the best for their new family.

There's a story that Gaga tells about her parents as a young couple. One day, they were relaxing at Joe's parents' home, and they saw a strange point of light in the air. It moved around the room and then disappeared into Cynthia's abdomen. Neither of them knew what they had seen, and they were mystified. The death of Joe's sister Joanne came to their minds, recalls Gaga. A sweet and creative girl, Joanne was only 19 when lupus took her life a few years earlier. If she was an angel now, had Joanne just given them her blessing?

Both Joe and Cynthia Germanotta worked hard in the telecommunications field. With their financial success, they were able to make a comfortable life for their family. They bought a fine townhouse in uptown New York, on the Upper West Side of Manhattan. "I grew up on 70th street, upper west side, right by Lincoln Center," Gaga told talk show host David Letterman in May 2011. "So I grew up across the street from the opera and the ballet, and I used to dream of being a star."

Speaking of her childhood, Gaga said in an interview that even when she was a small child, she was "a very provocative young lady."[1] When babysitters came to the house, Stefani made a point of leaping out of hiding stark naked, to surprise them. No wonder her parents gave their little left-handed daughter the nickname Loopy.

MOTHER LOVE

Gaga wrote about her mother in the lyrics for her song "Born This Way." "She rolled my hair and put my lipstick on / In the glass of her boudoir." When writing the song, she remembered that her mother had told her God made her and she was beautiful. Childhood memories like this were bright for young Stefani.

Mother and daughter had quiet times together. To this day, the singer's preferred cups for drinking are china teacups. They remind her of times when she and her mother used to drink tea together.

"My parents are really wonderful people and they always taught me to be loving and giving," Gaga told journalist Ben Mulroney when he asked about her childhood on an *eTalk* television special. "And the other part is that it's my destiny. I always had gay friends. I grew up with a culture of friends who were blind to culture, race, and religion."

There's a common childhood experience that *Rolling Stone* journalist Neil Strauss finds among the celebrities he has interviewed. "People who were raised and didn't have unconditional love from at least one parent are the ones who get involved in big-time scandals, who really become public spectacles once they get famous, because they just don't have that grounding and that stability," he believes. In his opinion, because of going without parental love, these celebrities are missing something important even when they are at the pinnacle of success. "They're less able to handle it, they're so needy for that love, they start doing stupid things. That's your Courtney Loves, your Britney Spears, that's your Paris Hiltons and all that."[2]

If Strauss is right, then there is something very clear about Lady Gaga. Since her late teens, she has been a working performer. Instead of the arrests for public drunkenness, criminal charges, and scandals that dog some celebrities, nearly all of Gaga's excesses and spectacles are merely costumes and performance sets. That is almost wholesome. It seems that this young entertainer is not craving approval that was missing at home. Her parents gave her the unconditional love that children need. Through their hard work and dedication, the Germanottas made a stable family home. That lasting security keeps this mercurial artist grounded.

MUSIC LESSONS

There was a record player in the living room of the Germanotta home. Joe Germanotta played records regularly, albums by Pink Floyd, the Beatles, and Billy Joel. He would pick up little Stefani and twirl with her around the room. They sang and danced along with Bruce Springsteen albums. There was a little plastic cassette player for Stefani's very own use, and she had her own collection of cassette tapes recorded by 1980s pop stars. For her, singing along with Cyndi Lauper and Michael Jackson was fun.

When Stefani was small, her parents had a piano for their living room. That first piano is still remembered and used by Gaga when she visits her parents. She commented on Twitter that she "wrote YOU and I in 10 minutes on the piano I learned on in NY. A boy dared me to write a hit."[3]

There are reports in tabloid interviews that Lady Gaga taught herself to play the piano, all by herself, when she was very young. "The self-generated myth that she'd learned to play the piano at age four—by ear—is another fabrication," according to biographer Maureen Callahan. She quotes Gaga as saying, "When I was four, my mom sent me to a piano teacher—she came to the house—[and] I really hated it. . . . I didn't want to learn how to read music, or practice." Her mother Cynthia, she recalled, "wanted me to be a cultured young woman. She would make me sit at the piano for two hours. So I could just sit there, or I could play."[4]

Sometimes her time at the piano was just playing with the sounds, but Stefani learned her lessons as well. Eventually the instruction included classical piano lessons. That teacher had Stefani playing scales with her wrists tied together, reported writer Lisa Robinson.

Music lessons continued throughout Stefani's childhood, and so did her daily practice. Playing by ear pleased Stefani more than reading music. That learning style lasted into adulthood. As a working professional, Lady Gaga is like many professional musicians who compose and arrange mostly playing by ear with only moderate skill at reading sheet music.

But as a child, her talent was only emerging. Her parents wanted to support their child's growing abilities. One of the ways they encouraged Stefani's creativity was to enroll her in Creative Arts Camp and other extracurricular activities. They had to find some way to tell whether Stefani was truly interested in music. With the birth of Natali in 1992, they now had two children to provide for. Their income wouldn't stretch to allow frivolous luxuries that would be abandoned if Stefani lost interest in music.

"My father gave me for Christmas the Bruce Springsteen songbook for the piano. And on it was 'Thunder Road' which is my favorite Bruce Springsteen song," Gaga said in an interview for an MTV special. Her father told her, "If you learn to play this song, we will take out a loan for a grand piano."[5]

The challenge was very appropriate. All in the Germanotta family were familiar with Bruce Springsteen's music. They knew what "Thunder Road" sounded like as "The Boss" performed it on his recording. The song wasn't a simple finger exercise for beginners. If Stefani learned to play that song, her parents would be able to tell if she was playing it well.

"So it was the hardest thing for me," Gaga said of her younger self, facing that challenge. When she opened up the book, the sheet music was more confusing than she expected. It wasn't what she was used to from her piano lessons. What were these guitar chords as well? It took her a while to understand what she was seeing. "I just started to read it and eventually got it down."[6] True to his word, Joe Germanotta took out a loan so that the family could have a fine piano. It was a baby grand, not a full-sized grand piano, Gaga acknowledges, but she didn't know the difference then.

That piano still occupies a central place in the Germanotta town house in uptown New York. When her two trophies arrived in January from the Grammy awards in 2010, they were delivered to her parents' home. Gaga posted a Twitter update with a link to a picture of the trophies, and crowed: "My dad put them on the piano I studied on for 14 yrs."[7]

A NATURAL VOICE

Singing was natural for Stefani. Members of her family sang in the shower, but she sang a lot of the time. She sang around the house, she sang for her friends and family. On fire escapes, she would dance and sing, pretending that she was a star. When the family was out in restaurants, she'd sometimes sing and drum on the table with breadsticks. This kind of behavior might not be expected in some families, but many Italian American families find it familiar. Some people have a taste for loud conversation or singing alone or together, at home and in public. As a young teenager, Stefani was not shy or self-conscious about singing where other people could hear.

She was singing to herself one day, while wandering in a store in downtown New York. She didn't realize that anyone was listening.

When a clerk came up to her, he told her she had a great voice. He also gave her his uncle's business card. His uncle wasn't just anyone—he was voice coach Don Lawrence.

Lawrence has coached Mick Jagger, Bono, Christina Aguilera, Axl Rose, and many other singers. He's been called "the vocal coach of the stars"[8] by at least one of the many artists and groups he has helped. Many professionals request his time and advice. It was a landmark day for Stefani when Lawrence made time to listen to her sing and give her advice for training her voice.

After hearing Stefani for himself, Lawrence praised her potential. It was Lawrence who suggested that she should start writing songs. The idea had immediate appeal for Stefani. Before long, she had written her first song, about losing love. Looking back on that first song, Gaga speaks of it with tolerance and humor. In interviews, Gaga has said that she wonders what she ever thought she knew about falling in love at the age of 13. That inexperience didn't hold her back. All through her teens, she kept on writing songs.

"I wrote HAIR about how my parents used to get pissed at my outfits and my hair when I was a kid,"[9] Gaga said on Twitter. When she was a teenager, for a while Stefani was a fan of the music of the Grateful Dead. At this time, she didn't keep her hair as sleek and neat as her mother preferred. She was trying to grow dreadlocks, but her fine, dark blonde hair wouldn't matt into proper dreads. When Stefani's hair got too rough, sometimes her mother would come into her room while she was sleeping and trim the dead ends of her hair.

"I was always an entertainer. I was a ham as a little girl and I'm a ham today," said Lady Gaga, when she was 23, on her website. "I always loved rock and pop and theatre. When I discovered Queen and David Bowie is when it really came together for me and I realized I could do all three."[10]

EAST SIDE STORY

When people want to go where fun and exciting things are happening in New York City, tourists might take a cab to Times Square. But residents and natives of New York know that the Lower East Side is where to go for music, restaurants, and art events. "The iconic East Village has been home to all walks of artists, musicians, actors, authors and intellectuals for years," commented an ad in *Vanity Fair*. The original gritty nature of the area has been glossed a little by gentrification, but there's still plenty to see. "A bar at every corner, a restaurant on every block . . . the East Village is also renowned for live music venues . . . [and] live performances of every ilk."[11]

Though the Germanotta family lived in a fine townhouse on the Upper West Side of the island of Manhattan, Stefani had access by public transit to the Lower East Side as well. In a matter of minutes, subways and buses could take her 70 or more blocks away from her neighborhood with her home, school, and familiar places like pizzerias. She knew the way, going on her own and with friends, to find interesting places to shop and hang out. "She says she was a 'bad' girl who snuck out of her parents' house to go downtown to Smalls and Arthur's tavern to see 'what was going on,'"[12] wrote a reporter for *Vanity Fair*. But dating wasn't one of the options at first. At her father's insistence, Stefani did not go out on dates until she was 16.

HELICOPTER PARENTS

There was no stage mother in young Stefani's life, pushing the young girl to perform to fulfill the mother's failed dreams. There was no manager father hustling his children through a working schedule that consumes their entire childhood. Instead, it seems more that her parents bought into Stefani's dream wholeheartedly.

"Her parents not only encouraged their daughter's ambition, but were so actively involved in her burgeoning career that they seem to be among the first generation of 'helicopter parents,'" wrote one reviewer.[13] The image of the helicopter is an apt one. Picture the parents hovering over their grown child, excessively attentive.

Cynthia Germanotta made many trips to nightclubs, escorting her teenage daughter. Together, they attended many open mic nights and amateur nights, looking for ways to get Stefani onstage performing. That's a parenting choice not many families would make. It might seem more natural for a parent investing in a child's dream to take the teenager to music tutors and all-age performances instead.

"She knew that I was going to sneak out, so she decided that she would chaperone," Gaga said on *Late Night with David Letterman*, the day her second album was released. "There was no stopping me, so my mom was really supportive. I've been doing this for a long time, so I've had lots of rejection. I feel really grateful to be here on David Letterman!"

What kind of mother begs nightclub managers to let her underage daughter perform onstage? The kind who believes in her daughter's dream. The kind who honestly believes the daughter will be protected from harm. This belief was almost a magical belief. And in fact, the meteoric rise to stardom was almost magical in a series of good luck. It just didn't happen as quickly as the Germanottas hoped it might, when Stefani was 14, or 15 . . . or 17, or 19.

Either or both parents accompanied their underage daughter to her performances. They carried her gear, usually an electric keyboard and speaker. If a full house was needed for the event, Cynthia would call on members of their extended family. There would be enough butts in seats to please the manager.

Joe Germanotta made no secret of using his business connections to arrange for auditions with music industry executives. Even the former business manager of Madonna, Bert Padell, consented to an audition with the teenage Stefani. Before that interview, Cynthia Germanotta did her own self-assigned homework. Carefully, she learned everything she could about Padell. The man wrote poetry, she told her daughter.

At the audition, a couple of polite questions about his poetry led to Padell giving the Germanottas a copy of his book of poems. He may have been touched or flattered at their interest in his poetry. But after watching Stefani perform, Padell merely wished her good luck with everything and said that he would call. For him, this was simply one of many auditions with unknown performers.

Some of Stefani's many auditions did pay off. When she was 15, Stefani appeared on an episode of television series *The Sopranos*. She played a rebellious teenager, and even had a few lines of dialogue. Her hair was its natural dark honey blonde, light brown.

HIGH-SCHOOL MUSICAL

At the private high school of the Convent of the Sacred Heart, the performing arts were not neglected. There were theater and music classes, and other activities at Regis High. "Stefani was always part of school plays and musicals," one of her former classmates was quoted as saying, in a *New York Post* article. "She had a core group of friends; she was a good student. She liked boys a lot, but singing was No. 1."[14]

One of the musicals in which Stefani played a female lead was *Guys and Dolls*, where she played Adelaide, the long-suffering fiancée of gambler Nathan Detroit. It's a demanding role, requiring a nasal voice using an accent derived from either Jersey or the Bronx, whichever seems funnier to the director. To native New Yorkers, the accent is a reliable comedic element in the production! It's no surprise that using different accents continues to be an ongoing part of Lady Gaga's performances.

For the school production of *A Funny Thing Happened on the Way to the Forum*, Stefani played Philia, a sweet-tempered virgin in a notorious Roman brothel. At the climax of the musical, Philia and two other characters are dressed similarly. All three run on-and offstage repeatedly in a comedy of mistaken identities. Though the high school was associated with a convent school, the theater program didn't shy away from productions with a sexual theme.

WORK IT!

During her sophomore year in high school, Stefani took on other challenges besides songwriting and performing. "I got three jobs waitressing," Gaga told many interviewers who asked about her past. "I was good at serving Italian food in heels."[15]

In a May 2011 interview, David Letterman asked Gaga, "What kind of waitress were you?" "A very bad one," Gaga admitted. "I used to flirt with everybody so that I would get tips. Except it didn't work so good if they were on a date. Not so smart."

Any career waitress will tell you, waiting on tables is hard on the feet. Trying to wait on tables while wearing high-heeled shoes adds to the pain. But Stefani had her reasons. She wore high heels not only because she was short. She stood just an inch taller than five feet. Wearing the shoes appealed to her, not only as a boost up to a more average height, but also because she liked the way the shoes looked. High-heeled shoes were the current fashion. And she noticed that customers tipped her more—much more—when she wore heels.

This fact was part of how Stefani began to realize what the customers noticed more than the service she was providing and the food that was prepared. People were also noticing how she looked and dressed. It was a lesson that Stefani later learned to apply in the nightclubs where she played at open mic nights.

SWEET 16

For Stefani's 16th birthday, her parents hosted a sweet 16 party. Joe and Cynthia rented a large hall for their daughter's coming-out party, and crowded it with good food and drink and music for the guests. Everyone was given a copy of a CD recording as a present—a demo recording by Stefani. It was clear to everyone attending that this was only the first of the galas that Stefani was going to have in a brilliant future. She was going places. She was going to be a singer and songwriter, and they could all say they knew her when she was starting out.

There was no car for a 16th birthday present for Stefani. Learning to drive is common for about half the teenagers growing up in various cities and towns across North America. But in New York City, the teenagers in middle-class and wealthy families often do not have cars of their own. Few young people learn to drive in this crowded, sprawling city. Stefani wasn't the only person in her circle of friends who didn't know how to drive. They got around by bus, subway, and transit trains, which are all more affordable than taxicabs. It made a big impression on her when she began dating, that one of her boyfriends had a turquoise car. Even by age 26, Lady Gaga still hadn't learned how to drive.

HIGH-SCHOOL CONFIDENTIAL

There are hints of what high school was like for Stefani. She felt like an outsider, but there are many photos of Stefani with her classmates. They dressed alike, in school uniforms or casual clothes. They looked alike in many ways, with long hair simply brushed. Their smiles are alike too: warm, uncomplicated, and cheerful.

Stefani didn't always feel uncomplicated, or similar to her classmates. "They used to call me rabbit teeth in school," she wrote in a Twitter note on February 5, 2011, adding, "and now I'm a real live VOGUE BEAUTY

QUEEN!" Her high-school dreams of success were coming true, as she crowed over seeing her own photo on the cover of *Vogue* magazine.

The yearbook from Stefani's senior year has several whimsical biographical facts about her laid out beneath a cute headshot. Her nickname? Stefi or The Germ. Her male equivalent was listed as Boy George. Her identical twin separated at birth? Well, that was obviously Britney Spears. It was well known at school that she had her heart set on becoming a pop star. Even then, her dream was listed as being a headliner at Madison Square Garden. The reality, according to her yearbook, would be Café Casa—it was no secret at school that while a sophomore, Stefi had worked as a waitress. And the listing ends with the observation that Stefi didn't make it to reunion, because she had an audition.

In interviews and during some concert performances, Gaga tells nostalgic stories of her high school years. "She even tells a funny story about smoking pot in the bushes behind the Met with her girlfriends when she was in high school," wrote Jonathan van Meter for *Vogue*. He was writing about a gala where Gaga performed, an event hosted by the Metropolitan Museum Costume Institute for their new exhibition "American Woman: Fashioning a National Identity." He added that everyone in the audience laughed when the singer quipped: "So I suppose it's kind of a triumph for me to be allowed inside tonight."[16]

There's a less happy memory as well. It comes from a day when Stefani went to meet friends for pizza at a restaurant near her home. Some girls who also went to school at the Convent of the Sacred Heart were at the same pizzeria, hanging out with some boys that Stefani knew. "The boys picked me up and threw me in the trashcan, on the street," Gaga said in an interview for an MTV television special. "On the corner of my block while all the other girls from the school were leaving and could see me in the trash. And everybody was laughing, and I was even laughing."[17] Her own laugh was a nervous giggle. *Don't let them see you cry*, she told herself, holding back tears and quivering lips. She'd rather laugh a little at her own situation than let them see her in tears.

"I remember even one of the girls looking at me like 'Are you about to cry? You're pathetic.'" That feeling stayed with her, of being seen as pathetic. What she recalls most of all after this event is that she just didn't talk about it to anybody. "I remember I didn't want to tell my parents because it was too embarrassing. And I remember I didn't want to really bring it up with my girlfriends even though they were there."[18]

Experiences like these bring strength to her songwriting, according to Gaga, and also help bring her closer to her fans. "I think that it didn't sink in with me how bullying affected me until later in my life," she said, looking back at her teenage years from the ripe old age of 25. "I knew that it affected me deeply, but it wasn't until a little bit later that I realized how much it affected me and how much it was still very present. I think it took me [to] get to know my fans and to see similar struggles in them for me to access that wound in myself," Gaga said soberly. "I think that my fans have been a key to my heart, unlocking things about myself that I didn't want to deal with, handle, or address. That makes me a greater songwriter."[19]

PEELING DOWN

After dozens of times onstage in small clubs, Stefani was fairly confident as a performer. She sang not only covers of popular songs, as some people did onstage, but her own compositions. Alone with her electronic keyboard, or backed up by a few friends, Stefani went onstage time and time again. Sometimes the crowd was salted with friends and relatives that her mother had phoned and badgered into attending. Sometimes the crowd was nearly all strangers. Native New Yorkers aren't gawking tourists, ready to be impressed by anyone. New Yorkers are cooler than wide-eyed tourists. It takes a lot more to impress them. And if a performer hasn't made a good impression in the first few moments, the club audience members often end up chatting quietly among themselves while waiting for *a real singer* to come onstage.

It was frustrating for Stefani, the times when she didn't have the audience's attention. Her voice was not astonishingly good, and her lyrics were not amazingly powerful. After a few bars of a song, sometimes the audience would let its attention wander. But she didn't let that inattention get to her or make her quit. The moment that made Stefani a performer who learned how to get and keep the attention of her audience was both a step forward into her future and a step back into her past. It came one evening when the crowd was talking and not paying enough attention to her song. She took off her clothes.

In her bra and panties, she sat back down on the piano bench and resumed her song. And this time, she had the attention of her audience. It didn't please her parents, but after she had done it, she knew that she'd gotten this group of strangers to look at her again. After that first time, she was willing to undress again if that's what it took to get people to stop talking and watch her.

Maybe Stefani was remembering how well getting naked had worked when she was a child, wanting to make a surprising entrance the first time a babysitter came to the house. "You're handed a certain set of baggage from your parents, your situation from growing up, etc.," commented journalist Neil Strauss when writing about his interview with Lady Gaga. "If you can get past that baggage and become yourself in this lifetime, then you've done a good job."[20]

Maybe Stefani undressed to remind her listeners that this was a real, live young woman only a few feet from their chairs, not a recording coming out of a speaker. Maybe she already felt exposed and vulnerable and wasn't going to pretend that she didn't. It could be that her emerging sexual nature gave her the confidence to display herself even more in front of the crowd. A British journalist later quoted her as being confident sexually. "'I'm a disaster with men,' says the beauty who was teased for being a lesbian at the strict Manhattan convent where she was educated. 'But I still believe I'm super-sexy.'"[21]

LOOKING BACK

How does Lady Gaga look back on her childhood, from the giddy heights of her popular success? With nostalgia and fondness. Singing on *Saturday Night Live* on October 3, 2009, she changed the lyrics for her song "Poker Face." It became an anthem about growing up in the city.

Wearing an outfit of orbiting metal haloes, she sang about Lenox Hill and cheering for the Yankees with her dad, but after traveling around the world she still prefers Rivington Street for drinking with her friends. Playing at a piano in front of a band that supported her after only a short rehearsal, she built a medley of two of her songs. Her lyrics were about missing the city of New York—subway trains, pretty girls, and cheap hot dogs. She sounded more than a little homesick for the past. But it was her confidence that rang clearest at the end of the song. "I was just a waitress on Cornelia, now I'm living my dreams, baby, singing 'bout my poker face."[22]

NOTES

1. Pastorek, Whitney. "Going GaGa." *Entertainment Weekly.* Posted February 6, 2009. Retrieved April 20, 2011. http://www.ew.com/ew/article/0,,20257096,00.html.

2. Brown, Molly. "Neil Strauss' Everyone Loves You When You're Dead." *Kirkus Reviews.* Posted March 15, 2011. Retrieved May 5, 2011. http://www.kirkusreviews.com/blog/question-and-answer/neil-strauss-everyone-loves-you-when-youre-dead/#continue_reading_post.

3. Lady Gaga. *Twitter.* Posted May 22, 2011. Retrieved May 24, 2011. http://twitter.com/#!/ladygaga.

4. Callahan, Maureen. *Poker Face: The Rise and Rise of Lady Gaga.* New York: Hyperion/HarperCollins, 2010, p. 21.

5. "Lady Gaga: Inside the Outside." MTV. Retrieved May 18, 2011. http://www.mtv.com/videos/news/653401/how-lady-gaga-learned-to-play-thunder-road.jhtml#id=1664075.

6. Ibid.

7. Lady Gaga. *Twitter.* Posted January 16, 2011. Retrieved April 10, 2011. http://twitter.com/ladygaga.

8. Murder, Jonny. "The Deadlyz." *SaYven Entertainment.* Retrieved May 4, 2011. http://www.facebook.com/TheDeadlyz.

9. Lady Gaga. *Twitter.* Posted May 22, 2011. Retrieved May 24, 2011. http://twitter.com/#!/ladygaga.

10. Lady Gaga. "Bio." *LadyGaga.com.* Retrieved February 20, 1011. http://www.ladygaga.com/bio/default.aspx.

11. Mastercard Advertising Section, "Sounds of The City." *Vanity Fair.* September 2010, p. 189.

12. Robinson, Lisa. "Lady Gaga's Cultural Revolution." *Vanity Fair.* September 2010, p. 280.

13. Callahan, *Poker Face,* p. 21.

14. Callahan, Maureen, and Sara Stewart. "Who's That Lady?" *New York Post.* Posted January 21, 2010. Retrieved June 20, 2011. http://

www.nypost.com/p/entertainment/music/who_that_lady_CBlHI927d
RlLmIwjVfGrwK#ixzz1S7qTAztz.

15. Parvis, Sarah. *Lady Gaga*. Kansas City, MO: Downtown Book-
works/Andrews McMeel Publishing, 2010, p. 15.

16. Van Meter, Jonathan. "Oprah Goes Gaga." *Vogue*. July 2011,
p. 120.

17. MacKenzie, Carina Adly. "Lady Gaga on Teen Bullying: The
Boys Threw Me in the Trash Can." *Pop2It*. Posted May 18, 2011. Retrieved May 18, 2011. http://blog.zap2it.com/pop2it/2011/05/lady-
gaga-on-teen-bullying-the-boys-threw-me-in-the-trashcan.html.

18. Ibid.

19. "Lady Gaga: Inside the Outside," *MTV*.

20. Brown, "Neil Strauss' Everyone Loves You When You're Dead."

21. Wight, Douglas. "Lady GaGa: LSD and Coke Drove Me Gaga."
News of the World. Posted February 7, 2010. Retrieved April 10, 2011.
http://www.newsoftheworld.co.uk/notw/showbiz/721084/LSD-and-
coke-drove-me-Gagabut-I-was-saved-by-ghost-of-my-dead-auntie-
Lady-Gaga-Drugs.html. Page no longer available.

22. Conklin, Mike. "Lady Gaga on *SNL*: Much Better Than U2 on
SNL." *The Measure*. Posted October 5, 2009. Retrieved May 18, 2011.
http://www.thelmagazine.com/TheMeasure/archives/2009/10/05/lady-
gaga-on-snl-much-better-than-u2-on-snl.

Chapter 3

"I'VE GOT THE SICKEST AMBITION"

The transformation seems complete. The brunette Catholic schoolgirl from the Upper West Side of New York City has seamlessly become an international pop idol. Her makeup is perfect, even to the addition of fake moles, or a highlighting of the real mole below her right eye. Her hair is bleached blonde or dyed aqua, or hidden under towering wigs. Haute couture and costumes clothe her body, still rounded, but now lithe. She puts on a serene manner as she calls her fans beautiful, and little monsters, with affection.

"But there was a time," wrote biographer Lizzy Goodman, "when this preternaturally composed young artist was just another self-described 'delusionally ambitious' kid from New York with a head full of dreams that contrasted starkly with her reality."[1] Young Stefani Germanotta got her education in music, formally in university as well as by singing and paying her dues in as a small-time professional in small performance venues.

FAKE IT TILL YOU MAKE IT

One of the traits that Lady Gaga has in common with her earlier self is behaving like a famous person. "When you're 16 and there's a line of people down the block at a nightclub, and you have the audacity to walk right in? That's my gift," Gaga told reporter Whitney Pastorek. "My gift is that people see something artistic and special about me. And you're gonna f**king watch."[2]

At 16 and 17, Stefani already saw herself as the professional performer that she wanted to become. Not everybody saw her in the same light, however. There's a quote from Lady Gaga posted on the community forum at *Billboard.com* magazine: "When I was 16 yrs old, I was way too weird to be on *American Idol*. They would've shut the door right in my face."[3]

"Obviously, when I wrote my album, I was not a famous person," Gaga said in February 2011 in an interview for 8TV, a Malaysian television station. "But my friends and I were all fascinated with celebrity culture. In our own way, we had our own celebrity culture, and hierarchy, in the scene in New York. It was sort of a heavy metal, party, hipster, '70s club culture. I like to say often that there's *lots* of Lady Gagas in New York. I'm just the one that got out."[4]

CO-ED ON CAMPUS

At 17, Stefani was accepted for early admission to New York University (NYU). That year, she was 1 of only 20 young people to be admitted to Tisch School of the Arts at NYU. She moved out of her parents' townhouse into a dormitory on NYU campus.

The time that Stefani spent in university was a welcome change from high school. She was glad to be studying in a co-educational campus, with male and female students, instead of an all-girl school. No longer required to wear a school uniform, she took pleasure in dressing the way she wanted, with more freedom. "Though she'd felt insecure in high school, Lady Gaga did not hold back in college," wrote biographer Sarah Parvis. "She wore crazy clothes and pursued her love of music."[5] Her outfits at this time, Gaga has said in interviews, got pretty wild. But some of her fellow students disagree when asked by journalists, saying that wearing suspenders with her jeans was about as wild as she dressed at that time.

Some of her written assignments have survived her time as a student, circulating out into the general public awareness. "I stumbled across a snippet of an essay that Gaga wrote while she was a student at the Tisch School of the Arts at New York University," wrote director Alistair Newton speaking about the production he wrote and directed, called *Of a Monstrous Child: A Gaga Musical.* "In it she explores transgressive sexuality, deformity and the social body, and the socio-political implications of nudity in North American culture—fascinating stuff."[6] But written assignments didn't fill Stefani's need to learn how to be the performer she wanted to become.

When she was attending classes at Tisch, Stefani hung out with other musicians who played together, and started a band that played her own songs and some cover tunes. The name of Stefani's band wasn't Wizard, like many heavy-metal wannabe bands across the continent. It wasn't a folk-rock collective name like The Byrds, either. She played keyboards and sang lead for the Stefani Germanotta Band (SGBand).

The members of her band changed as the months passed. Performing at small clubs on the Lower East Side, the SGBand caught the eye of Joe Vulpis, a music producer. The band did some recording in Vulpis's studio under a liquor store in New Jersey. Soon, the band's extended play recordings *Words* and *Red and Blue* were available and sold at their gigs wherever they performed in New York.

A few promo posters for *Red and Blue* can still be found by obsessive collectors. There are a few old videos of the SGBand, available on the Internet. The other members of the SGBand, shown playing drums, electric guitar, and bass in the videos, are all young men. They're all about Stefani's age, 17, or only a few years older. In one video, playing in front of a brick wall at a New York City club called The Bitter End, the band is comfortable with their skills but not brilliant. It is Stefani who is energetic, crouching at times over her keyboard.

STILL LOOKING

Higher education isn't available to everyone. Stefani knew that, and knew that attending Tisch was a rare privilege. Her studies in music were useful, and her songwriting skills became stronger through learning to write analytical papers and essays. But she wasn't really satisfied with what she was learning there. She kept taking auditions during her studies and won small parts. She felt more creative than some of her classmates, and that she had learned how to learn and think about art.

She left Tisch School of the Arts partway through her sophomore year. It just wasn't the way she wanted to learn. Her father agreed that she could try her way to make a career in music. He would even pay her rent for a year, but if she wasn't signed to a major record label by the time she was 20, she'd have to go back.

She hated the idea that she might fail at her dream. She was willing "to live the life of a starving artist,"[7] and put all her energies into succeeding as a working singer and songwriter. Even going back to NYU to study music seemed to her like a failure. Success as a recording star, singing and songwriting, was the only kind of success that she wanted.

Away from school and her family, Stefani got the cheapest apartment she could find. In the summer of 2005, that was a tiny place on Rivington Street. Sparsely furnished, the apartment had a futon bed with a David Bowie poster over it, and her keyboard and music player occupied the main room. That was about it, but she didn't need more.

She hung out with friends and didn't let networking get in the way of having a good time. "My favorite wine is Frenzia!!! Red," Gaga sent in a nostalgic Twitter message a few years later. "My gfs and I like to mix it with 7up and Marachino cherries. NY HOOKER BEVERAGE!"[8]

Because Stefani was willing to dance in a go-go dancer's cage and sing in any club that would allow her onstage, new opportunities kept coming her way. Her friends and acquaintances had a variety of musical tastes. With the hip-hop singer Grandmaster Melle Mel, Stefani recorded some songs to go with a book for children. *The Portal in the Park*, by Cricket Casey, has been re-released in a version with the name Lady Gaga on the cover.

Sometimes she'd invite friends in and cook for all of them. "The rumors I am a dab hand in the kitchen are completely true. I come from an Italian family—what more can I say?" quipped Gaga in an interview. "I love to cook. I am really good at Italian food. So I make great meatballs, pasta, and all sorts. I love it. When I get the chance, I make a mean meal."[9]

DISCOVERED

One night in June 2006, a young woman named Wendy Starland caught up with the SGBand's performance at the New Songwriters Showcase in a club called The Cutting Room. Working as the talent scout for a music producer, Starland knew she'd found someone special. She took hold of Stefani by the arm and said that she was about to change her life. Her boss, producer Rob Fusari, wasn't happy to get Starland's call from the noisy club. But he had told Starland to keep on the lookout for a new young female singer whose recordings he could produce for marketing to a major record label.

Fusari wasn't impressed by what he heard over the phone. And meeting Stefani face-to-face didn't help at first. The leggings and sloppy hat she was wearing didn't make a good impression. To Fusari, she looked soft and rounded, not lean and intense. It wasn't until he heard Stefani sing that everything changed for him, and he immediately got a contract for her to sign. He had been a producer for Whitney Houston and for Destiny's Child, and he knew what *marketable* sounded like. It sounded like her.

It's no surprise that the song that caught the attention of Rob Fusari in audition was Gaga's own song "Hollywood." In one video recorded about this time and later posted on *YouTube*, her intent is all over her as she plays keyboard and sings, in front of her band. "Listen," she tries to growl in her youthful, soft voice. "I've got the sickest ambition . . ."[10]

There were other performers at The Bitter End or the Mercury Lounge who had better looks, or more musical training. In New York City alone, there were dozens if not hundreds of young women and young men with as much to offer in a performance as young Stefani with or without her band. The difference is that for her, there was nothing else that mattered.

A RECORDING CONTRACT

Working her way through the club scene had given Stefani some idea of just how hard the life of a working musician can be. She was ready to take on the world. Working hard with Rob Fusari and Wendy Starland, Stefani took their advice about improving her songs and writing new and better ones. The tone of her songs began to shift toward an electronic dance music style.

At Fusari's insistence, Stefani made a serious effort to lose some weight. When a woman is only one inch taller than five feet, 10 or 15 pounds make a big difference. Her weakness for junk food just couldn't be indulged in as much as she'd like. Delighted that she was taking an interest in her physical health, her father got her a membership in an Upper West Side gym.

The story of how she took the name Lady Gaga varies, depending on who tells it. Starland remembers coming up with the name at a marketing meeting. Fusari claimed that he was always singing the song "Radio Ga Ga" whenever Stefani arrived at his studio in New Jersey, and one day a text message sent on his phone garbled "Radio Ga Ga" into "Lady Gaga." "My producer, Rob Fusari, used to call me Gaga as a nickname. He said I had a very Freddie Mercury-esque quality to my performance," said Gaga on a video interview with 8TV. "I became known as Gaga in New York, so I kept it."[11]

Though Fusari began an unprofessionally romantic relationship with Gaga, he also put together several of her songs and got her writing new ones that caught the attention of Island Def Jam Recordings. The modest-sized company, based in New York City, decided to take a chance on Gaga. In September 2006, she was signed with Island Def Jam. The goal was that she would have an album ready in nine months. Everything seemed to be working out according to her plans. But to her dismay, after only three months she was dropped by the label, with barely any explanation.

The news was devastating. Gaga retreated to her parents' townhouse for the Christmas season, and kept returning there from time to time over the next several months when her tiny apartment just wasn't enough of a refuge. Friends would find her asking to stay overnight, just to feel someone near, not wanting to be alone.

It took many months for Gaga to grapple with getting dropped from Island Def Jam. If not the worst thing that had ever happened to her, it was the second worst. The worst thing she had known previously was when her little sister Natali had fallen out of a tree and broken her arm. But even that horrible day had solutions. There were no X-rays and hospitals for someone whose confidence has been battered.

SUBSTANCE ABUSE

After being dropped by Island Def Jam, Gaga retreated to her tiny apartment, listening to music and taking drugs. "My cocaine soundtrack was always the Cure. I would lock myself in my room and listen to 'Never Enough' on repeat while I did bags and bags of cocaine," a British tabloid journalist, Douglas Wight, quoted Gaga as saying. "It was about being an artist. I wasn't a lazy addict. I would make demo tapes and send them around. At the time I didn't think there was anything wrong with me, until my friends said, 'Are you doing this alone?' Um, yes. Me and my mirror."

Drinking with friends or taking drugs alone didn't take up all of Gaga's days or nights, even during this time of excess. There were still songs to be written, and she would do it. Her neighbors would see her stumbling upstairs in her leotards and high heels in the middle of the night, and some of them wondered if a call girl had moved into the building. But they couldn't see that inside her little apartment she was writing lyrics and making up melodies. Her home-recorded demos kept adding up, and she'd send them out. She'd practice making up her face, take cocaine, and take off the makeup to try a different style. Sometimes it was a lightning bolt like the one David Bowie wore on the album cover of *Aladdin Sane*.

Her father couldn't understand why she was using drugs. He couldn't even look at her during this time. When she got a tattoo, she hid it from him for months, knowing he'd be upset. Eventually, Gaga's interest in substance abuse waned. "All of the trauma I caused to myself," she told Neil Strauss when he interviewed her later for *Rolling Stone*. "There are some things that are so traumatic, I don't even fully remember them."[12]

Tabloid journalist Douglas Wight made much of Gaga's admission to biographer Helia Phoenix that she took LSD during that time. He wrote that "one of her scariest LSD trips left her convinced she had met Radiohead rocker Thom Yorke."[13] That meeting hadn't really happened, but it would have been a remarkable meeting of minds. This influential British rocker stated in a 2010 interview that "It will be only a matter of time—months rather than years—before the music business establishment completely folds. [It will be] no great loss to the world."[14]

Yorke also warned upcoming artists not to sign traditional record deals that would tie them to the sinking ship. It will be interesting one day if Yorke and Gaga ever do meet and discuss trends in the recording industry.

In spite of her time of excess, many of Gaga's friends recall her as being "a girl so driven that she rarely indulged in alcohol, let alone drugs—[who] applied herself with . . . rigor and discipline."[15] Dropping out of Tisch led to some bad decisions such as substance abuse. But it was also a time in which Gaga kept making new demo recordings and kept finding new places to perform.

"I thought I was gonna die," Gaga was quoted in a tabloid article. "I wanted to BE the artists I loved, like Mick Jagger and Andy Warhol—and I thought the only way to do it was to live the lifestyle. But then I realized my father's sister Joanne, who'd died at 19, had instilled her spirit in me. She was a painter and a poet—and I had a spiritual vision to finish her business." The tabloid observed that the singer's closest companion remains her dead aunt—and that later, in 2009, she dedicated the Fame Ball tour to her. "I never met her," Gaga acknowledged, "but she's been one of the most important figures in my life."[16]

BURLESQUE PERFORMANCE

One of the friends that she made at this time was a performer who used the name "Lady Starlight." A few years older than Gaga, Lady Starlight knew about confidence in performance. This sort of confidence was exactly what Gaga needed. Her relationship with Rob Fusari was not going to last. She had fallen for a bartender named Lüc Carl, and in her heart they were Sandy and Danny, the lovers from the musical *Grease*. But Carl had more confidence in his own future as a heavy-metal musician than in her musical career. Having a friend like Lady Starlight made her believe that she really could grab an audience's attention. Learning everything she could from Lady Starlight, Gaga dyed her hair black and increased the eccentric nature of her clothing and costumes.

Together Gaga and Lady Starlight formed a duo they called "Lady Gaga and the Starlight Revue." Their show toured clubs around lower Manhattan. They billed themselves as "The Ultimate Pop Burlesque Rockshow" and wore costumes they'd made from hot pants, bikinis, and feathered headdresses. While playing covers from other bands' successful tunes, usually heavy metal or Black Sabbath, the duo would sing and accent moments by lighting cans of hair spray.

The burlesque element of their show used scantily clad women as part of the vaudeville theater tradition, where performances assumed a form of storytelling. "The idea that you can deliver a complex narrative using pyro and tits was a revelation for Lady Gaga,"[17] wrote biographer Lizzy Goodman. That revelation has had a lasting influence on every aspect of Gaga's performances. Her songs aren't just audio experiences. When she appears onstage or films videos, and wears costumes for interviews and appearances, Gaga is creating burlesque performances. "She's telling a story every time," according to Goodman. "They're all narrative statements that when reenacted live in sexually suggestive, cerebral ways become pieces of pop art."[18]

The neo-burlesque act of "Lady Gaga and the Starlight Revue" was generating enough good buzz that in August 2007 they were invited to perform at Lollapalooza in Chicago. Though she was not known at the national level, Gaga shared the stage with long-standing musical acts such as Pearl Jam, Daft Punk, Muse, Snow Patrol, and the Roots. She wasn't a headliner, of course. Her turn onstage came during the daytime. It didn't matter. She came onstage that hot summer day in a disco-ball bikini and black, thigh-high stockings.

The mirror tiles on that bikini were hand-glued in place by Gaga. At this time, Gaga's hair was long and dyed black. Many of the music fans gathered at Lollapalooza appreciated her looks and sound, but she wasn't generally recognized. In fact, many times during the festival she was mistaken for Amy Winehouse by that singer's fans. As for her sound at the event, there were some problems with the spinning of the recorded music, and Gaga was not happy. Lollapalooza was the end of her shared performances with Lady Starlight.

A NEW LABEL

Rob Fusari was still working on the songs that he and Gaga had created. Their big break came when his friend Vincent Herbert became the executive producer for Streamline Records, a new imprint of Interscope Records. Gaga was hired to write songs for performers on the

Streamline label, including Britney Spears, New Kids on the Block, Fergie, and the Pussycat Dolls. She sang a reference vocal for a track being recorded by singer-songwriter Akon, and he recognized the talent in her voice. Akon convinced the CEO of Interscope, Jimmy Iovine, to sign Gaga to Akon's own label Kon Live Distribution. By the end of 2007, Gaga was working with songwriter and producer RedOne. She also collaborated with Martin Kierszenbaum, another songwriter and producer at Interscope, and became part of his label Cherrytree Records. Together they wrote and recorded the songs that would become her first album.

It was good that Gaga had the support and expertise of experienced producers, because her association with Rob Fusari fell apart. Their relationship ended, and Fusari sued her, claiming that she had manipulated and exploited him.

Gaga's relationship with Lüc Carl wasn't thriving either. They broke up when she realized that he just didn't believe in her future as much as she did. He told her that she was delusional if she thought she was really going to make it big time.

That was it for Gaga. She demanded that he give her back the few things she kept at his apartment. One day, she told him, he wouldn't be able to get a cup of coffee at a corner deli without hearing about her.

LIVING A CALIFORNIA DREAM

When Gaga moved to Los Angeles in early 2008, it was with the plan of finishing her first album and its promotional videos. She settled in to do just that. After a going-away party in New York, a hungover Gaga got on a plane to Los Angeles. She went straight from the airport to the recording studio. There, in a matter of minutes she laid down the first tracks of the song that was to become her first hit, "Just Dance." Though it was a song about nothing more than dancing and drinking, it was also a focused effort to produce a surefire hit for Interscope. "[T]hat single was merely the opening salvo in what has pretty much become Gaga's breakout year,"[19] said an article in *Rolling Stone*.

In the bio on Gaga's website, the listing says that she "wrote all of her lyrics, all of her melodies, and played most of the synth work on her album *The Fame*."[20] Her producer was Nadir Khayat, also known as RedOne. His contributions became key to the emerging Lady Gaga sound. This Moroccan-born songwriter had moved to New York two years earlier when his song "Bamboo" came to global attention. "Bamboo" was picked by the Fédération Internationale de Football Association (FIFA) as the official melody for the 2006 FIFA World Cup. After making good impressions on the presidents of Epic Records and Interscope, RedOne became the co-writer and producer that Gaga needed to refine her songs.

The song "Just Dance" was presented to Interscope on February 8, 2008. That Friday, executive Jimmy Iovine kept a meeting waiting for him. Finally, he brought Gaga into the office where the meeting was held, and presented her to his entire team, telling her that she did everything that they had asked her to do, and now he knew why they had believed in her. Then he played "Just Dance" for the meeting, and Gaga danced on the boardroom table. It was a perfect moment of business and art celebrating together.

Several songs that she had written or co-written just weren't working for Gaga's own first album, *The Fame*. RedOne knew enough about the recording business not to keep these songs where they weren't working. Instead, these songs ended up being recorded by the Pussycat Dolls, New Kids on the Block, and Britney Spears.

The news of these recordings' financial success with other performers didn't make Gaga wish she'd released them instead. She had a contract as a singer-songwriter. Writing songs for other people was fine by her! This was part of her dream, to be a hard-working professional for a major record label. She had no problem seeing her song become a hit by Britney Spears. As for the Pussycat Dolls and New Kids on the Block, their producers and managers now knew Gaga existed. That acquaintance made it possible for Gaga to tour internationally with both these bands as a warm-up act later that year.

UNCONNECTED

The move to Los Angeles didn't end up being permanent. But then, nothing about Lady Gaga seems fixed or unchanging. Constant travel has become an element of her everyday life. Soon after relocating to the West Coast, Gaga began making regular visits back to New York.

She kept an apartment in Koreatown, a middle-class neighborhood of tract houses in the Los Angeles area, but it was New York that still felt like home.

"I put my toe in that water, and it was a Kegel-exercise vaginal reaction where I clenched and had to retract immediately," she told *Harper's Bazaar*. "I ran furiously back to New York, to my old apartment, and I hung out with my friends, and I went to the same bars."[21] The realization that New York City was home led to her writing the song "Marry the Night," which would be released a couple of years later.

The album was coming together. But her relationships with men weren't lasting. Few of the men she dated, like Brad Pitt, were able to handle the combination of her wildness and the time and effort she was putting into preparing her album and videos. "LA model Speed was dumped after he spotted her getting it on with Swedish male triplets on a sofa during a video shoot for [the] single 'Paparazzi,'" reported a British tabloid newspaper. "A source says: 'He started screaming at her on set.' Unsurprisingly they split."[22]

When she met Matthew Williams, something clicked for them both. They dated and broke up a couple of times over the next two years, but maintained a creative partnership that they called the *Haus of Gaga*. Totally trusting his artistic style, Gaga dubbed him "Dada."

The finished versions of her recordings became her debut album *The Fame*, which sold millions of copies overseas and in the United States. It also spawned three chart-topping singles, including "Just Dance" and "Poker Face."

THE BEST CALL

During a short visit back to New York, a phone call came for Gaga when she and her friend Brendan Sullivan were in midtown, eating lunch at a deli. It was a call that reversed the direction of all that self-promotion she had been doing for years. It was Bert Padell on the line, the former manager for Madonna, and *he* was calling *her*. He wanted to step in and take over as her business manager.

Years had gone by since Padell and Gaga had last spoken. Their one meeting hadn't really achieved anything. It had been merely one of the many auditions that a teenage Stefani Germanotta had done with high-level managers in the music business. Though she was now Lady Gaga, she hadn't forgotten that day.

"Actually, we have met," she told Padell smoothly. "My mother still has your book of poetry." That call was, as she told Sullivan, "the best phone call of my entire life."[23]

BOOMKACK AND BACKUP

Singing onstage is a visual performance, incorporating movement even for those singers who do not dance. And Lady Gaga does dance. Her "slightly f**ked-up"[24] moves, as she calls them, can be visually arresting. The performance of "Paparazzi" at the Grammy Awards was a classic example of how Gaga's moves, combining grace and stumbles, can rivet the attention of an audience. Her onstage movements are a tribute to the creative vision of her choreographer, Laurieann Gibson.

Soon after Gaga was signed to Interscope, she was introduced to Gibson, who became a key member of the *Haus of Gaga*, the creative collective that helped make Lady Gaga a breakout international sensation. "Back when the artist was dancing atop bars in seedy New York City nightclubs, Laurieann saw the star-power and brazenly predicted that she would sell 10 million—a record-setting feat that Lady Gaga recently surpassed within just one year and four months from her album's original release date," says a biographical essay on Gibson's website.[25]

Canadian-born Laurieann Gibson was classically trained, studying at the Alvin Ailey Dance Company. In New York City, she became a working dancer in hip-hop style with breakout artist Mary J. Blige. Gibson became a choreographer and creative director for Motown and Bad Boy Records. MTV's hit show *Making The Band* hired Gibson in 2005 as the on-air choreographer-in-residence. One of her signature exclamations, "Boomkack!" became a familiar part of that show.

It's not only award-winning videos for Lady Gaga that keep Gibson at the top of today's music industry. The Capezio design company chose Gibson to be the new face for their first hip-hop dancewear collection, Frontline dancewear. Gibson is also headlining "The Pulse" multicity tour of intense dance instructional seminars.

Gibson determines how Lady Gaga moves and is seen, onstage and in videos. The dance moves are choreographed, even the "signature stumble dance."[26] It's Gibson who shows Gaga how to move among backup dancers who may be called on to handle gracefully the train of Gaga's dress, 16 feet or longer. Gaga relies on Gibson's vision and guidance, and refers to her in Twitter updates as "my sister Boom-kack."

The backup dancers are not a faceless crowd when Lady Gaga performs. Even when their faces are covered by masks, the dancers are identifiable and recognizable. A casual survey of her music videos, concert footage, and *Gagavision* excerpts will show a series of dancers who become familiar. The troupe of regulars includes men with shaven chests and strong-muscled women standing a head taller than Gaga.

It's no wonder that Gaga can move with these dancers in videos and stage performances as confidently as if they were all her closest friends or lovers. These dancers are not new assemblies of professionals gathered for each tour or film session. Some of these dancers have worked with choreographer Laurieann Gibson for years now. They contribute

Lady Gaga performs in concert at Radio City Music Hall in New York City, January 2010. (AP Photo/Evan Agostini)

to the visual experience not only with their motions but the way they interact with Gaga. And when the moves are done, they breathe in cadence with her as the applause swells.

THE MESSAGE

"My goal as an artist is to funnel a pop record to a world in a very interesting way," Gaga wrote on her website. "I almost want to trick people into hanging with something that is really cool with a pop song. It's almost like the spoonful of sugar and I'm the medicine."[27] The messages behind the performances of Gaga include many references from popular culture. Some of the visual images are adult, sexual, and disturbing. Others are childlike, direct, and meant to teach. It isn't every pop star who can bite the head off a Barbie doll onstage, and also quote Julie Andrews in the role of Mary Poppins.

"Actively cultivating a gay following, as a performer, says two things," according to Maureen Callahan. "You are open-minded and nondiscriminatory, and you know that a gay fan base not only tends to be incredibly loyal but quite often ahead of the mainstream curve."[28]

In a 2009 interview for *Entertainment Weekly*, Gaga said then that she wasn't overly concerned with the way people receive her work. What she wanted more than anything was to do something important. "So what's important about, say, riding someone's disco stick?" asked the reporter. Her reply was: "It's sexually empowering women."[29]

"*The Fame* is about how anyone can feel famous," Gaga explains on her website. "Pop culture is art. It doesn't make you cool to hate pop culture, so I embraced it and you hear it all over *The Fame*. But, it's a sharable fame. I want to invite you all to the party. I want people to feel a part of this lifestyle."[30]

THE PERSONA

How real is the transformation from the schoolgirl Stefani to the superstar Lady Gaga? It seems like a consistent change, and an authentic development of her adult self, at least to observers.

Gaga isn't the only performer making the rounds these days who changed her name and look as a teenager reaching for the stars. A couple of years ago, a young girl named Robyn Fenty went through a similar time of transition. She put her trained musical talent to good use and wasn't afraid to showcase her good looks and firm, rounded body. The result? She's now a rhythm and blues singing sensation, using her middle name: Rihanna.

"Robyn is the brick to my foundation," the young singer said in an interview. "People know Rihanna from my music. But if this were to all go away tomorrow, I would think of myself as Robyn. But the life of Rihanna is pretty f**kin' awesome,"[31] she admitted.

"To her, 'Rihanna' is just a stage, like puberty, that started in a recording studio six years ago and will last however long it lasts," wrote Josh Eelis for *Rolling Stone*. "Meanwhile, she thinks of herself as Robyn."[32] The name Rihanna is used when she is working—onstage, in recording studios, filming videos, and giving interviews. It's still an effort for her to answer and respond when that name is called. But her parents and friends still call her Robyn. For this performer, the stage name Rihanna is only the name of the role she plays. It's not her entire self.

That's how she differs from Lady Gaga. It is no effort for Gaga to answer to that name, because she has invested a great deal of her self in that identity. The name her parents and friends call her, most of the time, is Gaga. From them, it's an affectionate nickname. It's also what they call her in moments of exasperation or anger.

TO THE TOP

There was nothing really wrong with Lady Gaga's musical career when she lost her contract with Island Def Jam. Compared with the careers of thousands of other working songwriters and performers across the United States, she was doing well. At that time, her earnings as a performer made it possible for her to live in New York City, where living costs are much higher than in most American cities. If she was also being financially supported by her parents, well, that isn't unusual for a young person. Gaga kept herself busy in her burlesque performances and preparing new demo recordings of her own songs. She had a working career, even if she felt it wasn't enough. Her ambition was to be a superstar.

Even with talent, there was no way to be sure that Gaga would make it all the way to the top ranks of celebrity pop stars. "Real success is still a long shot for a new artist today," said rocker Courtney Love in 2000. "Of the 32,000 new releases each year, only 250 sell more than 10,000 copies. And less than 30 go platinum."[33]

No one is really sure what makes the difference between an excellent recording that sells well and one that sells astonishingly well. Sometimes, it's the sound. Other times, it's clearly the message. Whatever quality a recording has, the top ranks of sales only occur when a song becomes wildly popular—and that can happen for any reason. "Actually, given the ready-made nature of her sound," suggested one analyst, "it's even more incredible that Gaga sold by-the-numbers dance tracks as mini-revolutions of the soul and a major revolution in the direction of pop music. It's a true feat of performance art."[34]

Part of the performance is that Gaga is always *on*. She is always turned on and ready to be seen and heard. Except when she is asleep, Gaga is always on show.

Another part of her performance is that she has always been on her way to the top. When she was a teenage wannabe, she behaved like a musical artist. By the time she was an emerging professional, she behaved as if she were a famous pop star already. She did the things she would have been doing if she were already successful—writing new songs and creating new performance material, and finding new places to perform. She was swanning her way into and out of restaurants and clubs and meetings as if everyone already knew her name and her latest song. "One thing I noticed is that people who are at the top and felt they deserved it, as much hubris as that is, often stayed there longer than those who got to the top and had doubts," commented journalist Neil Strauss. "One has to have some sense of deservedness and worthiness once one gets success."[35] And as she did become successful and famous, Gaga increased the intensity of her personal presentation.

There are a few performance sensations—the Sex Pistols, KLF— whose careers were created by marketing firms. Instead, Gaga is proud of paying her dues as a musical performer. "I did this the way you are supposed to. I played every club in New York City and I bombed in every club and then killed it in every club and I found myself as an artist," Gaga is quoted saying in her bio on her website. "I learned how to survive as an artist, get real, and how to fail and then figure out who

I was as singer and performer. And, I worked hard. . . . And now, I'm just trying to change the world one sequin at a time."[36]

NOTES

1. Goodman, Lizzy. "The Art of the Tease." *Lady Gaga: Critical Mass Fashion.* New York: St. Martin's Press, 2010, p. 15.

2. Pastorek, Whitney. "Going GaGa." *Entertainment Weekly.* Posted February 6, 2009. Retrieved April 20, 2011. http://www.ew.com/ew/article/0,,20257096,00.html.

3. Julie. "Billboarddotcom." *Twitter.* Posted May 12, 2011. Retrieved May 12, 2011. http://twitter.com/#!/Billboarddotcom.

4. LadyGagaBeforeM. "Lady Gaga Interview 8TV Quickie Malaysia." *8TV Quickie.* Posted February 10, 2011. Retrieved March 24, 2011. http://wn.com/8TV_Quickie.

5. Parvis, Sarah. *Lady Gaga.* Kansas City, MO: Downtown Bookworks/Andrews McMeel Publishing, 2010, p. 15.

6. Nestruck, J. Kelly. "Rhubarb Festival: Lady Gaga Gets a Musical of Sorts." Arts. *The Globe and Mail.* Posted February 16, 2011. Retrieved February 21, 2011. http://www.theglobeandmail.com/news/arts/theatre/nestruck-on-theatre/rhubarb-festival-lady-gaga-gets-a-musical-of-sorts/article1910318/.

7. Parvis, *Lady Gaga,* p. 15.

8. Lady Gaga. *Twitter.* Posted May 22, 2011. Retrieved May 24, 2011. http://twitter.com/#!/ladygaga.

9. Parvis, *Lady Gaga,* p. 16.

10. Germanotta, Stefani. *YouTube.* Retrieved March 22, 2011. http://www.youtube.com/watch?v=3b5mgPmw2zw&feature=related.

11. LadyGagaBeforeM, "Lady Gaga Interview 8TV Quickie Malaysia."

12. Strauss, Neil. "New York Post review." *Neilstrauss.com.* Posted March 1, 2011. Retrieved July 20, 2011. http://www.neilstrauss.com/elywyd/.

13. Wight, Douglas. "Lady GaGa: LSD and Coke Drove Me Gaga." *News of the World.* Posted February 7, 2010. Retrieved April 10, 2011. http://www.newsoftheworld.co.uk/notw/showbiz/721084/LSD-and-coke-drove-me-Gagabut-I-was-saved-by-ghost-of-my-dead-auntie-Lady-Gaga-Drugs.html. Page no longer available.

14. Yorke, Thom. "Radiohead—Yorke Warns Music Industry Will Collapse 'In Months.'" *Contact Music*. Posted June 9, 2010. Retrieved April 19, 2011. http://www.contactmusic.com/news.nsf/story/yorke-warns-music-industry-will-collapse-in-months_1145978/.

15. Callahan, Maureen. "Ditched." *Poker Face: The Rise and Rise of Lady Gaga*. New York: Hyperion/HarperCollins, 2010, p. 111.

16. Wight, "Lady GaGa."

17. Goodman, "The Art of the Tease," p. 16.

18. Ibid., p. 16.

19. "Grammys Will Not Let Gaga Compete for Best New Artist." *Rolling Stone*. Posted November 23, 2009. Retrieved April 15, 2011. http://www.rollingstone.com/music/news/grammys-will-not-let-lady-gaga-compete-for-best-new-artist-20091123.

20. Lady Gaga. "Bio." *Lady Gaga*. Retrieved February 27, 2011. www.ladygaga.com/bio/default.aspx.

21. Us Weekly. "Lady Gaga Says She Will Never Get Plastic Surgery." *Rolling Stone*. Posted April 13, 2011. Retrieved April 15, 2011. http://www.rollingstone.com/music/news/lady-gaga-says-she-will-never-get-plastic-surgery-20110413.

22. Wight, "Lady GaGa."

23. Callahan, "Ditched," p. 113.

24. Zee, Joe. "Lady Gaga—an Exclusive Interview with ELLE's January Cover Girl." *ELLE*. Posted December 2, 2009. Retrieved April 29, 2011. http://www.elle.com/Pop-Culture/Cover-Shoots/Lady-Gaga.

25. Administrator. "Bio." *Boomkack*. Posted April 8, 2011. Retrieved April 10, 2011. http://boomkack.com/web/index.php?option=com_content&view=article&id=69&Itemid=140.

26. Zee, "Lady Gaga—an Exclusive Interview with ELLE's January Cover Girl."

27. Lady Gaga, "Bio."

28. Callahan, Maureen. "Art of the Steal." *Poker Face: The Rise and Rise of Lady Gaga*. New York: Hyperion/HarperCollins, 2010, p. 80.

29. Pastorek, "Going GaGa."

30. Lady Gaga, "Bio."

31. Eelis, Josh. "Queen of Pain." *Rolling Stone*. April 14, 2011, p. 40.

32. Ibid.

33. Love, Courtney. "Courtney Love Does the Math." *Salon*. Posted June 14, 2000. Retrieved April 21, 2010. http://www.salon.com/technology/feature/2000/06/14/love.

34. Callahan, "Art of the Steal," p. 81.

35. Brown, Molly. "Neil Strauss' Everyone Loves You When You're Dead." *Kirkus Reviews*. Posted March 15, 2011. Retrieved May 5, 2011. http://www.kirkusreviews.com/blog/question-and-answer/neil-strauss-everyone-loves-you-when-youre-dead/#continue_reading_post.

36. Lady Gaga, "Bio."

Chapter 4

METEORIC RISE

Since emerging as a wildly successful professional singer in the public eye, Lady Gaga is constantly being asked what she's planning to do next. "My history is already written," Gaga told a reporter in November 2009, when asked what she had planned for 2010. "For me, it's already April of next year. I've designed everything I'm doing until then. It's finished. I feel as though the past two years have been training, and now I'm going to show everybody what I can do."[1]

WRITING FOR INTERSCOPE

"In my earlier days of writing for myself, I wanted songs to be more complex. I thought they had to be for me to be taken seriously as an artist. But writing for other people, you get to learn things about yourself and take on their insecurities," said Gaga when trying to describe the experience of writing songs meant for other artists to perform. "Now I can appreciate and incorporate more simplicity in lyrics and melody."[2] There are many professional writers who compose songs for performers to record. Most songwriters are simply not professional singers for several reasons. For instance, they might not have the temperament for performing in front of audiences. The management system for most record labels generally is set up to work with songwriters separately and differently from how they work with singers. In cases like these, separate does not mean equal or equitable. "I always looked forward to a little conflict with management," said singer-songwriter Steve Earle, when looking back on his own career. Like Gaga, he exercised dual talents. "We were making art. It was worth it for the art."[3]

TOURING WITH NEW KIDS ON THE BLOCK

The first tour that Gaga did after being signed to Interscope Records was a small promotional tour in clubs. It was a good start, but she wanted more. When Gaga made friends with Mario Lavandeira (aka blogger Perez Hilton), it gave a big boost to her publicity. "She likes to be two steps ahead of everyone else," Hilton says. "The only way to do that is to be plugged in and aware of what everyone else is doing and what people are thinking and what they're responding to."[4]

She was lucky to be chosen for the opening act for the reunion tour of New Kids on the Block. Band member Donnie Wahlberg went to see her live in Las Vegas for the Perez Hilton's Bash on July 4, 2008, and convinced his bandmates to pick Lady Gaga to be their opening act.

With the *Haus of Gaga*, she put together a brand new show. The stage held a DJ table for Space Cowboy along with three moveable LCD screens for her short videos. Four male dancers, trained by Laurieann Gibson, were Gaga's backup onstage. Her usual costume was either the white version of the Origami Dress or the black one, made of large crystal shapes, worn with the Haus headset from her performance at the 57th Miss Universe Pageant. For most of the tour dates, Gaga would perform two shows, one in a venue with New Kids on the Block and the other in a club to earn the money needed to pay for her tour props.

The craving for junk food that plagued Stefani in her late teens became less of a problem as Gaga went on tour. She tries to eat healthy snacks much of the time now. "She always asks for hummus backstage at her shows," reported writer Posy Edwards. "She loves Gummy Worms, too."[5]

HEELS OR BAREFOOT

There's no compromising when it comes to shoes for Lady Gaga. Her choice is to wear high heels at almost every opportunity that she will be seen publicly. Usually there are high platforms as well as heels. Designers have taken to loaning or giving her their newest designs. Gaga has been photographed in astonishingly impractical shoes and boots of various kinds.

For the *Tonight Show with Jay Leno*, Gaga was scheduled to appear on January 9, 2009, and sing "Just Dance." Unfortunately, there was a problem backstage: her shoes were missing. These weren't just any shoes, but a special pair designed by Christian Louboutin.

It's easy to identify any shoes designed by Christian Louboutin. Since 1992, his shoes have all had one thing in common—red soles. These lacquered red soles have even been registered as a trademark.[6] At a glance, anyone who knows the meaning of a red sole would know that this pair of shoes wasn't just some bargain-store pair left in the dressing room by a busy assistant.

The show was delayed for over an hour while a search was made, but it became apparent that someone had stolen the shoes. The shoes, costing over a thousand dollars, were not to be found. "But the show must go on, and *The Fame* diva was ultimately forced to perform her set barefoot," crowed a celebrity footwear website. "And without pants."[7] No substitutes were accepted by Gaga, who did the performance barefoot rather than compromise on her shoes. Wearing no pants over her leotard and stockings was a long-standing costume decision.

WHERE DO YOU GET YOUR IDEAS?

Pop music is often seen as mere filler for radio broadcasts. The music played in elevators is generally instrumental versions of mild-mannered pop songs from days gone by. In spite of her tense dance performances and artistic costumes, Gaga is not a shock-rock performer. She's not creating the music for a futuristic science fiction thriller. Make no mistake about it—what Gaga composes and performs are pop songs. Popular music, lowest common denominator, flavor of the month.

"Her moniker comes from Queen's 1984 hit 'Radio Ga Ga,' and like the song says, the girl is pure radio goo goo, radio blah blah . . . which suits her fine," wrote reporter Whitney Pastorek. "I don't make underground music that's passing for pop music," Gaga told Pastorek in early 2009. "I make unabashed pop music. I sit at the piano and think to myself, 'Find it, Gaga. What's that killer chorus?' It's not about what I'm *feeeeeel*ing."[8] The result is a killer chorus like "I want to take a ride on your disco stick" or "want your bad romance."

Through 2009, Gaga kept composing pop songs even while on an international tour, opening for the Pussycat Dolls. While on tour, calls to home were a lifeline for her. It seemed she was working all the time, going from concert to media interviews, and it was hard to get any rest. Her stage manager's wife became a good friend and would often let Gaga sleep beside her for company when she was lonely and overtired. If it was necessary to take Gaga to a doctor for vitamin shots and rehydration IVs, the manager or his wife would call her family to let them know she was overstressed and taking the morning off to rest.

Calling home didn't always put Gaga's mind at ease. Her father's heart condition worsened to the point where his doctor recommended immediate surgery. He refused to consider having an operation, preferring to let nature take its course.

Thinking that her father might die was terrifying for Gaga. She called him and begged him to have the operation. There was nothing she could think to say to convince him.

The next day, she stayed with her keyboard all day, playing and writing the lyrics for what became her song "Speechless." Most of the songs she had been writing as a songwriter for Interscope were not personal stories about her own deep feelings. Instead, she found herself writing lyrics asking if her father could be fixed if he broke. She didn't know what they could say if they ever talked again together. "Some men may follow me / But you choose 'death and company.'"[9] Eventually, her father did consent to the operation and let her pay for it.

Another family crisis that Gaga had to face later was when her grandfather Giuseppe Germanotta was dying. Her parents called her to come home from touring, and she visited him in a nursing home in New Jersey. Afterwards, sitting with her dad, they traded shots and talked about the past and future. She had to leave for England to rejoin her tour, but Gaga kept her grandfather in mind. She wrote a song, "Glory," about what she was feeling and played it during a transatlantic phone call. It's important to her that she believes he heard and understood the song. While much of what she composes is a market-driven art form, sometimes the songs that Lady Gaga writes are all about what she is feeling.

THE MOMENT OF TRANSITION

Behaving as if she were already a superstar is something that this performer has done since before she became known as Lady Gaga. But when did that superstar identity become real? Her career had a gradual progression from an unknown working performer to a celebrity. The transition from a celebrity to a superstar was nowhere near so gradual. If one performance tipped her over into the realm of legend, it was probably on September 13, 2009, when she performed "Paparazzi" at the 2009 MTV Video Music Awards. Arriving in a limousine with Kermit the Frog, Gaga left the puppet in the limo when she walked the red carpet in a stunning, feathered outfit with a steampunk style. During the ceremony, she sat with her father.

Gaga was the first performer that evening. Her song was presented at first as a frivolous little pop song. All in white, Gaga lay across the stage, in a visual homage to Madonna's own breakthrough performance at the Video Music Awards, singing "Like a Virgin" in 1984. Gaga sang with intensity while her dancers writhed furiously around her, costumed in white and lace. One male dancer wore a lace thong as a facemask. A female dancer came onstage in a wheelchair as Gaga gripped a crutch. Still dancing, she shed part of her costume and suddenly looked less built-up and armored in lace. Her bare stomach quivered. Halfway through the song, Gaga sat at the keyboard of a white piano. She played the middle eight bars, shaking the white curls of her wig like a mad thing. Jerry Lee Lewis would have recognized her pumping energy as her left hand pounded out the bass line. She even propped one foot on the keyboard.

At that point, the film broadcast of the event showed a cutaway shot of the audience, P. Diddy in particular. His mouth was hanging open in confusion and amazement. Then the camera cut back to Gaga scrambling to center stage, suddenly dripping in blood. It was fake blood, from a prop concealed under her bodice, but for a moment the bleeding looked horribly real. She kept on singing the final chorus, smearing her stained hand across her face. As she artfully collapsed, her dancers gathered around to hide her during one last choked gasp.

Then Gaga was lifted by rope above the stage, completing the illusion that she was bleeding and hanging to death. One of her biographers, Maureen Callahan, called this moment "her pop-culture suicide for fame," adding: "She even managed to make the white of her right eye look like it was bleeding. That's commitment."[10]

GAGA'S IDOLS

"Have you met any of your heroes?" asked reporter Graeme Thomson in 2009. "I met Grace Jones," Gaga replied. "It was a wonderful experience, she's an incredible woman, and I got to spend a little bit of time with her. It was so nice. I've been really honored by some of the people I've met, but I don't like to discuss it because it takes away the sacredness."[11]

Vanity Fair reported that on meeting Carole King backstage at a concert, Gaga burst into tears. Their meeting was a surprise and a pleasure for Gaga. King's career as a songwriter and a performer was an inspiration for the teenage Stefani harboring dreams of stardom as a pop singer. She wept with awe at meeting one of her idols, a woman who had shown her that it was indeed possible for a woman to work cranking out new tunes for the recording industry, and still produce quality material. To have the respect of one of her icons meant a great deal to Gaga.

STAYING IN MOTION

On tour with the Pussycat Dolls in England in April 2009, Gaga carried a china teacup everywhere she went. The British tabloids loved the idea, running photographs of her holding the cup. Articles about the teacup appeared in the tabloids and blogs as well. One story focused on the evening that Gaga went to dinner in Soho and left her teacup behind at a restaurant called Hakkasan. After a frantic phone call, the cup was returned to her. It didn't appear to be a unique or unusual teacup to the restaurant staff. Drinking from china teacups makes her feel grounded and reminds her of drinking tea with her mother.

As soon as she finished touring with the Pussycat Dolls in 2009, Gaga began planning a new tour. Together, she and rapper Kanye West intended to have a tour with high-energy concerts where they would each sing solo as well as duets.

"Just two weeks after Kanye West and Lady Gaga announced their full slate of 'Fame Kills' dates, the tour has been canceled. No official reason has been given for the cancellation, but ticket refunds will be available," reported *Rolling Stone* that October. "After the backlash surrounding Kanye's outburst during Taylor Swift's VMAs acceptance speech, the tour was rumored to be embattled. Now official confirmation of the cancellation comes from concert promoters Live Nation."[12]

Without missing a beat, Gaga and her team began planning instead her own tour to promote her album *The Fame*. She began a series of highly publicized events, including debuting her song "Bad Romance" at Alexander McQueen's new show of his fashion design. The Fame Ball tour began selling tickets as soon as dates were announced.

THE REAL THING

"Photographers say, I want to see the real you. What the hell are you looking for? I'm right here," Gaga said to Anderson Cooper, the host of *60 Minutes*. "You've seen me with no make up, you asked me about my drug history and my parents. This is exactly what I'm really like," Gaga insisted. She held up a china teacup. "This is the cup I drink out of every day. This is the diamond I put in my coffee." She dropped the brilliant-cut glass gem, the size of a cherry, into her drink. "It's not a real diamond," she admitted.

A little clumsy, she drank off the last of the coffee and managed to take the gem into her mouth. It was a childlike action, showing off in front of the *60 Minutes* cameras, but it wasn't impulsive. It looked like a plan to appear charming, and to disarm her viewers and Cooper. It was also a reference to the moment in the video for her song "Alejandro," where Gaga, dressed almost like a nun in a red vinyl habit, takes a rosary into her mouth.

"Have you struggled with any of those outfits?" a British reporter once asked her. "God yeah. I arrived recently for a show and the stylist had brought this outfit and the damn thing was like f**king 100 lbs—head to toe, leather, studs," Gaga exclaimed. "And I was wearing this famous Vidal Sassoon haircut where only one eye is showing. So basically I did this whole show carrying 100 lbs, looking out of one eye, dancing—and then my tits explode at the end. It's not as easy as it looks!"[13]

ADMIRATION FROM COLLEAGUES

Some performers feel that the music scene has been dominated over the last several years by young women who try to outdo each other, using sexy lyrics and sexier attire. R&B singer Melanie Fiona finds this trend to be less than effective than musical training.

"I feel like what is happening, in my opinion, is that everybody is trying to outdo everyone else in fashion, in racy lyrics, in your style. Just be yourself and people will appreciate your individuality more," said Fiona in an interview with *Rap-Up TV*. "Someone who I really admire in this industry is Lady Gaga 'cause Lady Gaga has been Lady Gaga forever. When you're the real deal, you are who you are. What she's based in is true classical training and real vocal ability and a performer."[14]

As a music critic, Alistair Newton found Gaga's performances in Toronto refreshingly different from what he's seen before at music events and concerts, saying, "Lady Gaga offers a very welcome if rather extreme earnestness and passion. In the face of banal hipster 'authenticity' and icy detachment, I salute her for it." When asked if "Born This Way" was a good song, Newton had this to say: "The fact that she got the word 'transgendered' into a mainstream pop hit that is currently going number one all over the world makes up for some of the other dodgy lyrics and lame appropriation of Madonna . . . Camille Paglia be damned."[15]

Another music critic wrote for the *New York Times* that "Born This Way" was "flawless mimicry of late-1980s Madonna. From anyone else it would seem like a rip-off, but from her, it's a provocation, a dare," said Jon Caramanica. "Maybe there's as much meaning in excavating someone else's past as in excavating your own."[16]

No less a hard-rock icon than Sammy Hagar has praise for Lady Gaga. The singer and guitarist Hagar was the front man for the band Van Halen for years, before his solo career. The Red Rocker thinks that younger music fans are interested in rock and roll again, and rock stars too.

"In the 1970s and in the '80's you could have had your choice [of rock stars] between David Bowie or Robert Plant or Roger Daltrey or Pete Townshend. They lived it and brought it to you, and had the mystique. And you believed it and paid to see it," Hagar said in an interview. "But, then, Lady Gaga is a rock star. I think there's no question about that. She might be the new David Bowie."[17] At 63 years, Hagar was fronting his own band Chickenfoot at the 2011 Canadian Music Week festival in Toronto, Ontario.

Meanwhile, across town from the festival, Gaga's Monster Ball tour filled an arena with 20,000 screaming fans. Her new song "You and I" was delivered with a swaggering beat that suggests Gaga may be learning something from the songs of Elton John. "Her flaming-fingered lead guitarist dished solos at regular intervals during the show," commented a Canadian music critic, "which also featured a couple of flashy turns by Canadian violinist Judy Kang, playing a pink electric violin."[18]

"The girl, who turns 25 on March 28, sure knows how to work it," wrote Denis Armstrong for the *Ottawa Citizen*, "with a monstrously entertaining show that blended Broadway-scale gospel service and fashion show in a strip joint with semi-naked vampires modeling costumes by Gaga's own *Haus of Gaga* for an otherworldly experience that put George Lucas to shame."[19]

PRAISE FROM THE PRINCE OF DARKNESS

The music business is different now than it was before the end of the millennium, according to rock star Ozzy Osbourne. At 61, Osbourne is showing the effects of neurological problems and a lifetime of excess, but he still keeps up with recent trends in music.

"It's completely different, they're manufactured people now . . . like ice cream," he said in a 2010 interview for CNN. "Every now and then somebody comes out and I really like them—I really like this Lady Gaga." As reported by writer Scott Colothan, "The Black Sabbath legend believes Gaga is one of the few to stand out from the crowd in a music industry plagued by manufactured artists."[20] Few performers earn that much praise from the aging rocker.

NOT A FAN

On sports talk radio WFAN, comedian Jerry Seinfeld took time out during an interview to complain about Lady Gaga's then-recent behavior. At Citi Field during a June 2010 New York Mets game, Gaga attended the event wearing a studded leather bra—the one worn in her "Telephone" video. When paparazzi and fans buzzed around her, she flipped a raised middle finger their way. The spotlight had definitely moved away from the field where the Mets played.

The team's front office took advantage of a luxury box lying vacant to relocate Gaga and restore some order among the crowd. Unfortunately, the front office didn't take time to get permission from the person who had booked the luxury box for the season. That patron was Jerry Seinfeld, who is a lifelong fan of the Mets. "I can't believe they put her in my box," said Seinfeld on WFAN. "You give people the finger and you get upgraded? Is that the world we're living in now?" He did acknowledge her performance skills, saying "She is talented. I don't know why she's doing this stuff."[21]

Unlike Seinfeld, for Donny Osmond the problem is the sexual nature of Gaga's performances. The former teen heartthrob is quoted as saying that "he would not let his child watch one of her sexually provocative videos."[22] When he was a young performer, girls in the audience would squeal and swoon, but he did not indulge in mimed sexual moves onstage. For Osmond and his brothers, that sort of behavior felt inappropriate.

Gaga reads everything written about her, positive or negative, according to her makeup artist Billy Brasfield. "By facing your haters, you educate yourself about what people are saying," he says. "You take what you can learn from it, and f**k the rest of it."[23]

PRESENTATION

"Gaga makes outrageous declarations—which, when you break them down, actually make sense," admitted a critic for the LA Times. "And then she backs them up, not only through her now famously provocative interviews but in her videos, her collaborations with designers and artists, her live performances and those infernally catchy hits."[24]

Though Gaga gives polished, prepared interviews studded with sound bites, her true art is her performances. She performs her music with a distinctly visual element, both onstage and in videos. When discussing her video for "Bad Romance," Gaga made reference in interviews to ways that the entertainment industry is a metaphor for human trafficking. Human products are being sold. Performers, particularly women, are perceived as commodities on the market.

"She sounds more like an art critic than an evolving club kid," wrote journalist Ann Power. It's true that there are many examples of rockers and club kids who have art connections. But Powers points out that Gaga has done something more than make reference to her art school studies. "She's tapped into one of the primary obsessions of our age—the changing nature of the self in relation to technology, the ever-expanding media sphere, and that sense of always being in character and publicly visible that Gaga calls 'the fame'—and made it her own obsession, the subject of her songs and the basis of her persona."[25]

It's a cliché of popular culture that rock stars embody the social concerns of their age. They illustrate our shared anxieties. It's far less common for an artist to go under the skin and show the anatomy of our

Lady Gaga performs at a concert in Seoul, South Korea, August 9, 2009. (AP Photo/ Lee Jin-man)

shared fantasies and cultural delusions. In some of Gaga's costumes, the bones are on the outside.

"When she presents herself as a cartoon character or a space alien, she explores old questions about gender, artifice and 'reality' using the new language of social media, body modifications and transgender sexuality," according to Powers. "These deep issues are her tools, as important to her art as the glitter and latex in which she shrouds herself."[26]

"When I say to you, there is nobody like me, and there never was, that is a statement that I want every woman to feel and make about themselves," Gaga insists. "I don't make it as a defense. I make it as, OK, guys, it's been two years, and I've made a lot of music, and I know my greatness is individual. And I want every woman to be able to say that."[27]

GRADUATION CAMEO

"Never one to blend in with the crowd, all eyes were on Lady Gaga at her 18-year-old sister's graduation from the Convent of the Sacred Heart in Manhattan on Tuesday," wrote an online commentator for *Zimbio* in June 2010. "On a high school coolness scale of one to ten, having Lady Gaga as your big sis would have to be an eleven."

It didn't look like Natali Germanotta minded much when her sister's appearance at the high-school graduation ceremony was anything but subtle. There was no way that Gaga could blend into the crowd of parents and siblings, not in a sheer lace bodysuit and heel-less platform-soled boots, even if a black veil shrouded her face. A chauffeur whisked the star away from the crowd after the ceremony, but still, Gaga was there for her sister for one of the moments that count in a young person's transition to adulthood.

The younger Germanotta girl is no stranger to Gaga's fans. Her face is familiar after Natali played a cameo role as a prisoner in the video for "Telephone." There might be a future in performing for Natali, who "has been taking lessons with a top NYC vocal coach—paid for by Gaga, of course,"[28] reports the *Zimbio* commentator.

DO THE MATH

With all these performances and record sales, there's a lot of money being spent by Gaga's fans on concerts and albums. But the cost of her costumes and props is high, and her travel costs are astronomical. Is Lady Gaga actually making any money?

That's a fair question. Many singers and songwriters who work for major record labels have contracts that give the lion's share of profits to the label. "The system's set up so almost nobody gets paid,"[29] said rocker Courtney Love.

That statement was made in New York City in May 2000, at the Digital Hollywood online entertainment conference in New York City. The speech made by Courtney Love became a media sensation. Later, the speech appeared on *Salon.com* as an essay entitled "Courtney Love Does the Math." "Love not only excoriated the record industry for its fear of the Internet and its refusal to embrace the future; she also called them glorified slave-owners for their financial exploitation of artists," wrote nonfiction book author Maureen Callahan. While on tour, performers like Lady Gaga have many expenses to pay that can eat up all their earnings. "It was the latter point that made headlines: [Love] did the math, explaining how a band made up of four members, working with an advance of $1 million, would most likely, and through no fault of their own, wind up netting $45,000 each over the course of twelve months, while the label proportionally grossed $11 million and netted $6 million."[30]

As Love points out, major record labels are distributors of music recordings to stores. Without distributors, independent releases like *Red and Blue* from the SGBand are only available to customers at performances. Labels used to be the gatekeepers for the only way to get music recordings heard and sold. "Artists pay 95 percent of whatever we make to gatekeepers because we need gatekeepers to get our music heard. Because they have a system,"[31] she said. Love pointed out that when a major label decides to spend enough money promoting an artist, the label can occasionally push an artist to success through their system. All of the expense is recovered from that artist's album sales.

Because Love realized that she had basically been giving her music away for free under her contract with a record label, she wasn't afraid of learning how to work with alternative and online music markets. "Giving music away for free is what artists have been doing naturally all their lives," Love came to understand, even artists whose albums were sold in stores. "Record companies stand between artists and their fans.

We signed terrible deals with them because they controlled our access to the public."[32]

The stores aren't always much help to a musician, either. "I believe that monopolies, in terms of the music industry and artists having guns held to their heads for where they have to sell their albums, I think it's unfair," said Gaga in 2011 after breaking her agreement with the store chain Target. "It's unfair to us, it's unfair to the public."[33]

Love advocates for self-marketing and small record labels. She doesn't believe that singers and songwriters need gatekeepers any more, in order to get the music distributed to customers. As for Internet marketing skills, in May 2000 Love's 19-year-old webmistress was doing a better job of promoting and selling Love's recordings online than the record labels ever did.

On the other hand, Gaga's goal is to be not just a working music professional, but an international pop music superstar. For that kind of success and worldwide marketing, Gaga insisted on getting a contract with a major record label. After getting that contract, the *Haus of Gaga* kept her own website going strong.

Unlike the majority of singers whose music is distributed by a major record company, Gaga appears to be making a large income—at least, for now. No one can tell at this point if her success will be lasting. It would be smart for her to save what she can for the future. But *Entertainment Weekly* quoted Gaga as saying, "I spend all my money on wardrobe and props. I don't care about money."[34] After growing up in an affluent family, Gaga may not care about money now. And in the future, it may become important to her that her contract with Interscope sends half her income to her father.

BUBBLE WORLD

When interviewed for *New York* magazine in March 2010, the accent that Gaga used was very odd. There was no Bronx in it at all. The writer Vanessa Grigoriadis felt it was a combination of a robot and Madonna as Madge. The effect was increased over the two hours of the interview, because Gaga refused to remove her lightly tinted sunglasses. "What I've discovered," said Gaga in her robotic tone, with her head tilted for the camera, "is that in art, as in music, there's a lot of truth—and then there's a lie. The artist is essentially creating his work to make this lie a truth, but he slides it in amongst all the others. The tiny little lie is the moment I live for, my moment. It's the moment that the audience falls in love."[35]

During that spring, Gaga was very taken with her new "bubble dress." She and Grigoriadis talked about it being unreal, and beautiful because it seemed imaginary. The dress that everyone wanted was a bunch of plastic balls, not really a dress at all.

"On my tour," she declared, "I'm going to be in my bubble dress on a piano made of bubbles, singing about love and art and the future. I should like to make one person believe in that moment, and it would be worth every salt of a No. 1 record." At that point, Gaga dropped the accent and leaned in for a moment. She seemed more like a real girl, without that artifice. "I can have hit records all day, but who f**king cares?" she explained. "A year from now, I could go away, and people might say, 'Gosh, what ever happened to that girl who never wore pants?' But how wonderfully memorable 30 years from now, when they say, 'Do you remember Gaga and her bubbles?' Because, for a minute, everybody in that room will forget every sad, painful thing in their lives, and they'll just live in my bubble world."[36]

TIME GOES BY

The Monster Ball tour continued into 2011, with the same sets and costumes and an expanded set list including newly released songs. As the *Houston Press* noted in April 2011, "the show was the same but completely different than [sic] the one we saw last July. . . . OK, the merch was different, but that's a quibble."[37] Of course, there would be new souvenir merchandise, or merch, available as the tour continued. There's no way that the promotion machine surrounding Lady Gaga would miss opportunities for new marketing and profit.

The biggest change noticed by fans attending tour performances separated by a year or more in time was the change in how Gaga presented herself. To some, the performer seemed to be becoming more vicious than energetic. "Gaga seemed leaner and hungrier than last year's show," reported Craig Hlavaty. "She was on the prowl, not just traipsing through a set of columns and meeting dance and lighting cues."[38]

At this point, Gaga had been touring the Monster Ball show for almost two years. In some ways, performing onstage must have been like walking into a home studio every evening. The familiar walls and furnishings were all put together from the ground up in a new arena. Every performance took place in the same setting, but in another city each time. There could be a real sense of the familiar combined with the strange.

"And yeah, the whole storyline running through the show is corny," wrote a Houston reporter, "with a band of lithe, toned, and sweatily-attired misfits trying to get to this mythical 'ball,' but on this leg of the tour the plot has been largely abandoned for Gaga to take us to domina-trix church in between songs. She likes to scream."[39] There were 16 songs in the set list that night, with "Bad Romance" and "Born This Way" for the encore. That's a big increase from the six song sets Gaga was singing at the beginning of her time as an opening act for New Kids on the Block on their comeback tour.

"If you're on an island, stranded, and all you have is sticks and leaves and pineapples, you're gonna make a boat out of sticks and leaves and pineapples," Gaga explained to a writer from the LA Times. "I view glamour and celebrity life and these plastic assumptions as the pineap-ples. And I spend my career harvesting pineapples, and making pies and outfits and lipsticks that will free my fans from their stranded islands."[40]

SINKING IN

"Celebrity life and media culture are probably the most overbearing pop-cultural conditions that we as young people have to deal with, because it forces us to judge ourselves," observed Gaga in the LA Times. "I guess what I am trying to do is take the monster and turn the monster into a fairy tale."[41]

The grand goal Gaga had from her youth was to be a superstar pop singer, but it was also a little vague. How could superstar status be mea-sured on any objective scale? Sometimes there are watershed moments. About two weeks before an interview published in the September 2010 issue of Vanity Fair, Gaga realized that at that moment, she was actually the biggest pop star in the world. She was on tour in Australia, leaving a venue after a performance.

"I literally realized what had happened in my life," Gaga told reporter Lisa Robinson. She had just finished a two-hour concert, onstage before tens of thousands of fans assembled in the hot sunshine. Afterward, it took her nearly two hours to get ready to leave that location. As she got into a vehicle waiting to take her to the next appointment, her departure was noticed. Looking up, she could see there were some 5,000 people standing outside behind a perimeter fence, on stairways and platforms leading to a train station. She said, "Stop the car."

Then she got out of the car and walked out in the open. "The scream was so loud, it was a *roar*. I went over to the fence and signed as many autographs as I could without them pulling me through. More fans than ever had been waiting for me outside after the show," she marveled. In Australia's parching heat, the fans had waited two hours for a glimpse of her as she left. "It was *insane*. And then, I thought, How could I possibly be better for you? That's all I keep thinking: I just want to be better for you. I want to say and sing the right things for you, and I want to make that one melody that really saves your spirit that one day."[42]

NOTES

1. Thomson, Graeme. "Lady Gaga: The Future of Pop." *The Observer*. Posted November 29, 2009. Retrieved April 20, 2011. http://www.guardian.co.uk/music/2009/nov/29/lady-gaga-interview.

2. Edwards, Posy. "Making It." *Lady Gaga: Me & You*. London: Orion Books, 2010.

3. Earle, Steve. Q CBC Radio One. Broadcast April 29, 2011. http://www.cbc.ca/q/weekly/2011/04/26/this-week-on-q-46/.

4. Grigoriadis, Vanessa. "Growing Up Gaga." *New York*. Posted March 28, 2010. Retrieved June 30, 2011. http://nymag.com/arts/popmusic/features/65127/.

5. Edwards, Posy. "Meet Gaga." *Lady Gaga: Me & You*. London: Orion Books, 2010.

6. Christian Louboutin Trademark Application, Official Gazette. *Counterfeit Chic*. Posted July 10, 2007. Retrieved May 18, 2011. http://www.counterfeitchic.com/Images/Louboutin%20red%20sole%20in%20TM%20Official%20Gazette%207–10–07.pdf. Page no longer available.

7. Muller, Paige. "APB: Lady Gaga's Missing Christian Louboutins." *ShoeMinx.* Posted January 17, 2009. Retrieved April 22, 2011. http://shoeminx.com/apb-lady-gaga%E2%80%99s-missing-christian-louboutins/.

8. Pastorek, Whitney. "Going GaGa." *Entertainment Weekly.* Posted February 6, 2009. Retrieved April 20, 2011. http://www.ew.com/ew/article/0,,20257096,00.html.

9. Germanotta, Stefani. "Speechless." *LadyGaga.com.* Retrieved April 15, 2011. http://www.ladygaga.com/lyrics/default.aspx?tid=18497741.

10. Callahan, Maureen. "Offended Anatomy." *Poker Face: The Rise and Rise of Lady Gaga.* New York: Hyperion/HarperCollins, 2010, p. 197.

11. Thomson, "Lady Gaga."

12. "Kanye West and Lady Gaga 'Fame Kills' Tour Canceled." *Rolling Stone.* Posted October 1, 2009. Retrieved March 30, 2011. http://www.rollingstone.com/music/news/kanye-west-and-lady-gaga-fame-kills-tour-canceled-20091001.

13. Thomson, "Lady Gaga."

14. Rutter, C. J. "Melanie Fiona Admires Lady Gaga and Her 'Real Vocal Ability.'" *Tale Tela.* Posted March 31, 2011. Retrieved April 5, 2011. http://www.taletela.com/news/5830/melanie-fiona-admires-lady-gaga-and-her-real-vocal-ability.

15. Nestruck, J. Kelly. "Rhubarb Festival: Lady Gaga Gets a Musical of Sorts." Arts. *The Globe and Mail.* Posted February 16, 2011. Retrieved February 21, 2011. http://www.theglobeandmail.com/news/arts/theatre/nestruck-on-theatre/rhubarb-festival-lady-gaga-gets-a-musical-of-sorts/article1910318/.

16. Caramanica, Jon. "Pop Sirens Flirt with Today and Yesterday." *New York Times*, February 20, 2011, p. AR9.

17. Wheeler, Brad. "The Monday Q&A: Sammy Hagar." Globe Arts. *The Globe and Mail.* March 7, 2011, p. R3.

18. Everett-Green, Rupert. "Lurid, Bitter, Swaggering, Maternal—and Oddly Real." Globe Arts. *The Globe and Mail.* March 5, 2011, p. R2.

19. Armstrong, Denis. "Concert Review: Lady Gaga Scotiabank Place, Ottawa—March 7, 2011." *Jam.* Posted March 8, 2011. Retrieved March 13, 2011. http://jam.canoe.ca/Music/Artists/L/Lady_GaGa/Concert Reviews/2011/03/08/17532381.html.

20. Colothan, Scott. "Ozzy Osbourne: I Really Like Lady Gaga." *Gigwise*. Posted January 29, 2010. Retrieved April 5, 2011. http://www. gigwise.com/news/54377/Ozzy-Osbourne-I-Really-Like-Lady-Gaga.

21. Kreps, Daniel. "Jerry Seinfeld Calls Lady Gaga a Jerk." *Rolling Stone*. Posted June 23, 2010. Retrieved April 15, 2011. http://www.rollingstone.com/music/news/jerry-seinfeld-calls-lady-gaga-a-jerk-20100623.

22. Robinson, Lisa. "Lady Gaga's Cultural Revolution." *Vanity Fair*. September 2010, p. 280. http://ladygaga.wikia.com/wiki/Vanity_Fair_ (magazine).

23. Grigoriadis, "Growing Up Gaga."

24. Powers, Ann. "Frank Talk with Lady Gaga." *Los Angeles Times*. Posted December 13, 2009. Retrieved April 9, 2011. http://articles.latimes.com/2009/dec/13/entertainment/la-ca-lady-gaga13-2009dec13.

25. Ibid.

26. Ibid.

27. Ibid.

28. ahsanhussain. "Lady Gaga Upstages Kid Sis at High School Graduation." *Zimbio*. Posted June 11, 2010. Retrieved March 28, 2011. http://www.zimbio.com/Lady+Gaga's+Sister/articles/4LT5ht50_fU/ Lady+Gaga+Upstages+Kid+Sis+High+School+Graduation. Page no longer available.

29. Love, Courtney. "Courtney Love Does the Math." *Salon*. Posted June 14, 2000. Retrieved April 21, 2010. http://www.salon.com/technology/ feature/2000/06/14/love.

30. Callahan, Maureen. "Ditched." *Poker Face: The Rise and Rise of Lady Gaga*. New York: Hyperion/HarperCollins, 2010, p. 100.

31. Love, "Courtney Love Does the Math."

32. Ibid.

33. Christian. "Lady Gaga Takes Self-Portrait for the Advocate Cover Story." *Propagaga*. Posted July 5, 2011. Retrieved July 20, 2011. http://www.propagaga.com/2011/07/05/lady-gaga-takes-self-portrait-for-the-advocate-cover-story/#more-14977.

34. Pop Style. "Lady Gaga: 18 Outrageous Outfits." *Entertainment Weekly*. Posted February 4, 2010. Retrieved April 20, 2011. http://www. ew.com/ew/gallery/0,,20309550_20309885,00.html#20635417.

35. Grigoriadis, "Growing Up Gaga."

36. Ibid.

37. Hlavaty, Craig. "Friday Night: Lady Gaga at Toyota Center." *Houston Press Blogs*. Posted April 11, 2011. Retrieved April 18, 2011. http://blogs.houstonpress.com/rocks/2011/04/lady_gaga_toyota_center.php.

38. Ibid.

39. Ibid.

40. Powers, "Frank Talk with Lady Gaga."

41. Ibid.

42. Robinson, "Lady Gaga's Cultural Revolution."

Chapter 5

AWARDS CEREMONIES—GAGA FOR THE WIN!

When Lady Gaga makes an appearance at an award ceremony, the event becomes more than the public celebration it is for other celebrities. It becomes even more of a performance than the usual parade down the red carpet or showcasing of a few songs. The displays that Gaga makes at award ceremonies are strongly contrasted to her concerts and interviews. Each award ceremony has vaulted her media attention to new heights.

MAKING IT WORK

Any award ceremony that is televised becomes a news event. It's a great opportunity for performers to get publicity without having to buy airtime to broadcast their own shows. Of course, the performer must have an appropriate outfit, which isn't cheap. He or she must be able to hold the attention of the paparazzi while walking along the red carpet at the front door. As well, some performers are able to use their time onstage to springboard their careers to new levels of media attention.

"You don't have to be a superstar to execute a great PR stunt," observed communications consultant Mia Pearson, but being a superstar really helps. "With the right tactics, a focused strategy and a creative approach, stunts can be amazing tools for businesses of any size that are looking to inspire a crowd and create buzz around their brand. . . . The execution of a strong stunt is a delicate art: if done properly, the benefits can be huge, but if not, the public display could result in a PR disaster."[1]

After an event, the audience may not remember who won the awards, or for what. "We don't watch the MTV Video Music Awards for the awards, or even for the videos," wrote journalist Alex Strachan. "We watch for the music: the musical performances, the musical train wrecks and, on occasion, for those mad, made up 'MVAs Gone Wild' moments that have little to do with music but often involve musicians. . . . Nobody cares whether Lady Gaga won more VMAs last year (eight) than Eminem (two)."[2]

GRAND ENTRANCE

At MTV's September 13, 2009, Video Music Awards (VMA), Gaga arrived in a limousine, naturally. Her date was Kermit the Frog, but she left him behind in the car. Instead, it was her father who sat with her at the ceremony.

Her black lace dress that evening was designed by Jean Paul Gaultier. Accenting it were a wide-brimmed hat and a neck brace designed by Keko of London that added a brassy, steampunk look. The outfit was impractical, to say the least, but included an astonishing range of textures.

When she performed "Paparazzi" that evening, it was a showstopper. The white leotard she wore left her belly bare. The expressions on the faces of her audience ranged from astonishment to confusion, and at the end, the applause was thundering.

When she accepted the VMA for Best New Artist, Gaga came onstage in a red lace sheath over a G-string. Her face and head were masked in red lace and towering red spikes. Unable to speak in the mask, Gaga pulled it off so that she could thank God and the gays.

Before being photographed backstage with her award, Gaga slipped into a padded bodysuit designed by Gaultier that looked like a costume from a space opera. Sparkly black boots reaching to her knee completed that ensemble.

Seated in the audience again later that evening, Gaga wore a sequined sheath designed by Jean Paul Gaultier, and a feathered headdress circling her face. She wore the sequined dress to the after-party, but her headdress was different—an almost-bridal look of satin, lace, and pearls that she handcrafted herself.

There was a time when Gaga handmade all her costumes and accessories. For a while after she signed with Interscope Records, she continued to make her costumes and accessories with help from her associates in the *Haus of Gaga*. At first, when she or Matt Williams approached fashion designers for samples to wear, most designers refused. Others were surprised to learn that when they had loaned a gown or outfit to Williams or others it was used by Gaga for a photo shoot or an appearance. By 2010, many designers were willing and eager to dress Gaga.

BONDAGE GOTHIC

Performing at the American Music Awards in November 2009, Gaga made headlines with the Ace Bandage–adorned costume she wore.

Lady Gaga performs onstage at the 37th annual American Music Awards on November 22, 2009, in Los Angeles. (AP Photo/Matt Sayles)

What symbolism could be gathered from the bandage element of the costume? Gaga told an interviewer that the costume was meant to be feminine, with healing imagery from the bandages. It was meant to be a kind of bondage gothic. The healing imagery was less apparent than the padded replica bones hiding her face and parts of her body. The effect was more reminiscent of the facehugger from the 1979 motion picture *Alien*.

"Lady Gaga may have lost out to Gloriana for the Breakthrough Artist Award at last night's American Music Awards," commented *Rolling Stone* magazine the next day, "a loss so crushing, Gaga unleashed her anger by using a mic stand to smash a plate glass window during her AMAs performance."[3]

YOUR SONG

At the 52nd annual Grammy Awards on January 31, 2010, Gaga wore a total of six different outfits. On the red carpet, she arrived wearing an ensemble designed by Giorgio Armani. The hooped skirt dipped to the floor in the back and rose provocatively high in the front. Loops of stiff ribbon circled the skirt and bodice like crazy orbits of electrons or tiny rings around Saturn. In one hand, she held a long-rayed star. Her blonde hair, tipped with yellow paint, tumbled around her shoulders.

A short while later, the outfit she wore while being photographed backstage with her two awards had a short dress of prismatic material, an Armani Privé ensemble. The short dress was probably far more comfortable than the long gown she wore on the red carpet. The high platform-soled shoes were the same ones she had worn earlier with the science fiction gown, accented with rhinestones and soap bubble beads, as was the body stocking covering her arms and legs with similar beads. Keeping on the beaded body stocking was a good trick for making the quick dress change possible. Her spiky crystalline headdress made everyone walking near her take care not to lose an eye.

While performing at the awards, Gaga wore a green sequined leotard so tight and brief that her groin was compressed and displayed. After she was photographed in this leotard, there was an end to rumors about Gaga having a penis. She sang a medley of her songs "Speechless" and "Poker Face" with Sir Elton John and his own "Your Song." As they stood onstage together, the padded shoulders on her leotard rose higher than his head. In a theatrical moment, the singers entered part of the set labeled "Incinerator"—only to return onstage smudged with ashes and soot to sing again.

Before the event, the National Academy of Recording Arts and Sciences considered but ultimately did not make a rule change to make Gaga eligible for the Best New Artist category at the 2010 Grammys, even though her "Just Dance" was nominated for Best Dance Recording in 2009. The award that Gaga did take home was Favorite Female Singer in Pop/Rock Music.

PALE AS DEATH

Some of Gaga's red carpet arrivals are for galas and charity fundraisers, as well as awards ceremonies. The American Foundation for AIDS Research (amFAR) knew they could count on her to bring media attention to their events. It's impossible to be an advocate for gay rights, as Gaga is, without being aware of research into AIDS and HIV. February 10, 2010, saw Gaga on the red carpet at the amFAR Gala in New York. There her outfit consisted of a white leather jacket and hat worn with a white bikini. Her shoes were laced-up ankle boots with towering platform soles and heels. There was plenty of her bare skin showing, dusted with white paint and glued-on pearl beads.

Days later, she received three awards at the 2010 Brit Awards—Best International Artist, Best International Female, and Best International Album. Deeply affected by the recent suicide of her designer friend Alexander McQueen, Gaga honored his memory in her acceptance speech. At the ceremony, Gaga performed an acoustic medley of two of her songs, "Telephone" and "Dance in The Dark" in a calmer fashion than her usual high-strung style. She did not attend any parties after the awards ceremony. A year and a half later, when her album "Born This Way" was released, the song "Fashion of His Love" was dedicated to McQueen's memory.

McQueen's suicide in 2010 left his studio reeling. His longtime associate Sarah Burton stepped in as the head of design for the company that still bears his name. "He hated too many seams," Burton said of McQueen. "He always started with the form and knew everything about how to construct a garment. He felt he had to know everything about tailoring, everything about dressmaking. He'd always surprise us in fittings. We would tell him something was technically impossible—and in the morning there would be something amazing on the mannequin, even if he had to work all night to achieve it."[4]

"That Lady Gaga desired to be draped in McQueen's creations for her performances shows younger readers how significant he is in the fashion world," said a letter to the editor in *Vogue* magazine. "We fashion lovers will forever mourn the loss of this visionary."[5]

TOP OF HER GAME

Gaga attended the 2010 MTV VMA, appearing on the red carpet in a floor-length gown by Alexander McQueen, complete with a full black crinoline petticoat. McQueen also designed her sky-high platform shoes with spike heels. Nicknamed "armadillo shoes" by some, the footgear looked like they were covered in python skin. For headgear, she wore a brassy crest set with gilded feathers. Her companions were dressed in faux-diplomatic suits and wore stolid expressions.

Backstage, she shared a kiss of mutual congratulations with Laurieann Gibson, her choreographer, in mutual congratulations when "Bad Romance" won the award for Best Video. She took six awards in all, including Best Female. For her Best Pop Video acceptance speech, Gaga wore a black leather Armani gown with spikes on the breasts. Her spiky headgear this time was like a black Mohawk of spikes. Back at her seat, she drank from a teacup—this time glazed in black.

To accept the award for the Video of the Year, Gaga wore a meat dress designed by Franc Fernandez. As Gaga accepted the award from Cher, all eyes were on the flank steak swaying around Gaga's body. It was a new experience for Cher, to be upstaged by any other artist, but she took it well. When Gaga struggled with holding her purse and the award, Cher smiled indulgently. As Gaga reached for the microphone to accept the award with thanks, she ran out of hands and had to ask Cher for help. "I can't believe I'm asking Cher to hold my meat purse," said Gaga.

This wasn't the first dress made out of meat, though the media attention made the outfit seem absolutely astounding. There was an earlier dress designed by Montreal artist Jana Sterbak, which toured several countries and sparked many critical comments.

Lady Gaga poses backstage after accepting the award for Video of the Year for "Bad Romance" at the MTV Video Music Awards on September 12, 2010, in Los Angeles. (AP Photo/Chris Pizzello)

At the VMA in 2010, Gaga received 13 nominations in all, including 2 nominations in each of the categories Best Female Video, Best Collaboration, Best Pop Video, and Video of the Year. That set a new record for the VMA. At the ceremony she was awarded 8 of the "Moonmen" trophies, including Best Female Video, Best Collaboration, and Best Pop Video. After winning Video of the Year for "Bad Romance," Lady Gaga kept her promise to fans and revealed the title of her next album, to be released in 2011: *Born This Way.*

PERFORMANCE ART

It's pretty clear that Gaga's videos, concerts, and particularly her appearances at high-profile media events are meant to be a form of performance art. But the intent of the performance is not obvious. "Is this an expression of Lady Gaga's strength as a woman or an exercise in self-objectification?" asks Nancy Bauer, a philosophy professor. "It's hard to decide."

"Women of my generation have been scratching our heads," Bauer admits in an article she wrote for the *New York Times*. She's been trying to understand whether Gaga's presentations are part of a new attitude about women and feminism. "When we hear our daughters tell us that in between taking A.P. Statistics and fronting your own band you may be expected to perform a few oral sexual feats, we can't believe it."[6]

Bauer believes that the tension in Gaga's self-presentation is not just an idiosyncrasy or self-contradiction. That tension, she says, is the epitome of what life is like today for some young women who are comfortably affluent. "There's a reason they love Gaga. On the one hand, they have been raised to understand themselves according to the old American dream, one that used to be beyond women's grasp: the world is basically your oyster, and if you just believe in yourself, stay faithful to who you are, and work hard and cannily enough, you'll get the pearl. . . . The genius of Gaga is to make it seem obvious—more so than even Madonna once did—that feminine sexuality is the perfect shucking knife."[7]

Another commentator, Ann Powers, compares the performance art of Gaga to that of the artist Cindy Sherman. "Both draw our attention to the extent to which being a woman is a matter of artifice, of artful self-presentation," she says. "Gaga's gonzo wigs, her outrageous costumes, and her fondness for dousing herself in what looks like blood, are supposed to complicate what are otherwise conventionally sexualized performances."[8]

A FASHION ICON

In 2011, the Council of Fashion Designers of America (CFDA) awarded special tributes to honor several public figures—photographers, journalists, international icons, and founding figures. They decided to give their Fashion Icon Award to Lady Gaga, as a tribute to her being a fashion revolutionary impacting style today.

At the last possible minute, Gaga arrived at the awards ceremony. She swanned along the red carpet in her teetering high black boots designed by Noritaka Tatehana. The heel-less boots were swept by an immense train, so long that she simply could not find time and space to stand with the publicists before the show.

"Whether or not you think Gaga deserved the trophy, it felt like everyone in the room was just waiting for the awards preceding hers to hurry up and finish so she could take the stage," observed fashion writer Amy Odell. That was "a sentiment that really proved the CFDA made the perfect choice in Gaga for the fashion prize."[9]

The train was removed from her black outfit when Gaga came onstage to accept her trophy. And as she turned away from the microphone, it became apparent that there wasn't much back to the outfit, just sheer black panty hose over a thong. Walking offstage meant walking up a set of stairs in her heel-less platform shoes, with her "ass essentially bared to the most elite of the American fashion industry and doing it with grace surely deserved special recognition."[10]

KIND OF A DRAG

The performance to talk about at the 2011 MTV VMA was Lady Gaga's arrival in drag. For the entire event, she stayed in her persona as Jo Calderone, Jersey boy from a Sicilian family. "By the time her monologue entered the fourth minute, she had lost the crowd inside the venue, though she won everybody right back with her stout performance of 'Yoü and I,'" wrote commentator Kyle Anderson. "A little Jo Calderone goes a long way."[11]

The Calderone presence didn't end there, as she/he made appearances in two other segments of the show, during Gaga's win for Best Female Video as well as the tribute to Britney Spears. The drag performance almost eclipsed Beyoncé Knowles's announcement of her pregnancy. Tony Bennett's tribute to the late Amy Winehouse went almost un-mentioned in the press afterwards.

"You could argue that Gaga's decision to spend the night in her drag persona, 'Jo Calderone,' was awkward and annoying, a joke that went too long. And you'd be right," wrote commentator Darren Franich. "This was the rare instance in which Gaga did *not* fully commit to a look: She couldn't seem to decide how much she was playing her role, and in her later speeches she fell back and forth between being 'Jo' and being 'Gaga,'" said Franich. Still, he gave Gaga credit for doing something different without getting into some crazy robot-alien costume. In his opinion, Gaga as Jo had some of the best lines of the show. "Don't act like your TV didn't explode when she/he introduced Britney Spears by saying, 'I used to hang posters of her on my wall and touch myself.'"[12]

The feedback from viewers varied from annoyance to laughter. One commentator on *Entertainment Weekly*'s live blog noted that this was probably the longest time Gaga has ever spent in one outfit.

"The pop queen was infinitely dedicated to the act, as became apparent when she appeared in the VMA press room and would only answer questions as Calderone, despite being introduced by handlers as Lady Gaga," noted one reviewer. Even when asked by a journalist how one persona can inspire or affect the other, the performer dodged the question, saying: "She's just really f**king pissed at me right now and she said, 'F**k you. If you really love me, you'll go instead of me, and you'll get in that spotlight.' So I did."[13]

SMALL-SCALE CELEBRATIONS

It's not only at major awards ceremonies that Lady Gaga is turning heads. Sometimes just her music alone is the center of attention. Often her songs are covered by bands at small events, whether or not anyone would ever expect her musical style in that venue. There's a YouTube video[14] posted of an Orthodox Jewish wedding celebration, where the band plays a fanfare from Gaga's "Bad Romance." The vocalists replace her scat vocals with their own words in Hebrew and the name of the bride and groom. The brassy trumpets and sharply spoken lyrics are backed by a klezmer band in a surprisingly powerful moment.

That video is only one of many thousands of videos of similar events showing people of this heritage and other backgrounds. People around the world are enjoying Gaga's music and integrating it into their celebrations. The musical fusion shows that pop music is still a music of the people, a form of folk music. As a composer, Gaga is celebrating not only herself but life experiences that are understood by many people.

THE EGG

Looking to inspire a crowd and create a buzz, the stars arriving at the Grammy Awards (February 14, 2011) ran a gauntlet of cameras and journalists. The red carpet cleared for the passage of yet another sensation. But this time, it wasn't a sleek figure draped in a gown or a suit fitted by a master designer. This time, four strong young people with dancer's bodies swept along, scantily dressed. On their shoulders, they were holding a wooden frame supporting a large egg. Another dancer walked beside the egg, one hand raised to rest artfully upon the curve of the shell. Perhaps the shadow of her hand could be seen by a person who was just visible inside the cloudy, translucent plastic shell.

It was no secret who was concealed in that egg. It was Lady Gaga. She made her entrance in private splendor. Her bearers carried Gaga in her egg swiftly through the crowd, past the paparazzi to the backstage area. She wasn't there to sit among the attendees in their rows of seats. She was there to perform the opening act.

This egg delivery wasn't the first event of its kind in show business. "In 1990," remembered journalist Robert Spuhler, "a turkey mascot called the Gobbledy Gooker hatched out of a shell ringside at the WWF Survivor Series."[15] Still, Gaga's appearance beat that of the wrestling mascot, hands down.

Lady Gaga arrives at the 53rd annual Grammy Awards on February 13, 2011, in Los Angeles. (AP Photo/Chris Pizzello)

When the egg was brought onstage, it began to glow. As it opened, Gaga was revealed in a bare-midriff costume in egg-yolk yellow. With her dancers, she began to perform "Born This Way." And at the height of the song, during the middle eight, she climbed a stair to a keyboard set up with clear Plexiglas tubes like a fantasy organ. There, she played a few bars from the opening of Bach's "Toccata and Fugue in D minor"— the theme that's come to be iconic in classic horror film scenes, where the mad scientist exults in pride.

"No one knows how to grab attention better than Lady Gaga," said Cenk Uygur, one of two video journalists commenting on the event for *The Young Turks*, a web television talk show that has become the flagship of the TYT Network. "We've said it a million times."

"I would be one of those half-naked people," said Ana Kasparian, the other commentator. "I would love to be part of something like that. . . . Let me tell you, people are giving her harsh criticism for it," she added. "They're saying that she's stooped to a new low, calling her a fame-whore, right, that she's doing whatever she can to get that attention. No, good on her!" Kasparian insisted.

Uygur agreed, adding, "What are you supposed to do, sing in your basement? Come out of an egg in your basement? That doesn't do anybody any good." Both agreed that those who are complaining about Gaga's displays are just haters.

"She stole the Grammys, that's what she did," claimed Kasparian. "She went to all of those Grammy winners and said give me that, gimme that. No one's going to talk about *your* ass tomorrow. They're going to talk about *me*."

"Who won the Grammys? I dunno." Uygur shrugged. "I don't know *anyone* who won the Grammys. I know about the chick who came out of the egg. Genius. Gaga for the win!"[16]

It was expected that Lady Gaga would make some incredible fashion statement at this awards show. "It is always exciting to see what she and her designers will come up with next," commented journalist Mia Pearson. "But this time, something was different: chatter was focused not only on what she did, but why she did it. Everyone was asking the same question: 'Why an egg?'" Pearson pointed out that "Lady Gaga succeeded in making sure that all eyes were on her, cleverly carving out a space to talk about the meaning behind her new chart-topping song. What she and her team did was successfully pull of a brilliant PR stunt: not only do I have 'Born This Way' stuck in my head, but I (and people across the globe) now know all about the message and the intent of the music."[17]

The symbolism of the egg seemed obvious. Lady Gaga is no one-hit wonder. She's been in the public eye just long enough that it's clear she is more than just the flavor of the month. But to arrive at the Grammys in an egg symbolizes that she is still young and new as a performer. Her career is at its beginning.

NOTES

1. Pearson, Mia. "Could you pull off a Gaga-style stunt?" *Globe and Mail*. Posted February 17, 2011. Retrieved February 21, 2011. http://www.theglobeandmail.com/report-on-business/your-business/grow/mia-pearson/could-you-pull-off-a-gaga-style-stunt/article1911186/.

2. Strachan, Alex. "MTV Awards Just About Fun." *Victoria Times-Colonist*. August 28, 2011, p. C10.

3. "Grammys Will Not Let Gaga Compete for Best New Artist." *Rolling Stone*. Posted November 23, 2009. Retrieved April 15, 2011. http://www.rollingstone.com/music/news/grammys-will-not-let-lady-gaga-compete-for-best-new-artist-20091123.

4. Bowles, Hamish. "Noble Farewell." *Vogue*. July 2010, p. 142.

5. Tucker, Kendrick M. "Talking Back/Letters from Readers: McQueen of Hearts." *Vogue*. July 2010, p. 34.

6. Bauer, Nancy. "Lady Power." *Opinionator New York Times*. Posted June 20, 2010. Retrieved April 18, 2011. http://opinionator.blogs.nytimes.com/2010/06/20/lady-power/.

7. Ibid.

8. Ibid.

9. Odell, Amy. "Lady Gaga on Texting Anna Wintour, Anderson Cooper on Child Modeling, and More Highlights from the CFDA Awards." *New York Fashion*. Posted June 7, 2011. Retrieved June 7, 2011. http://nymag.com/daily/fashion/2011/06/lady_gaga_on_texting_anna_wint.html.

10. Ibid.

11. Anderson, Kyle. "Lady Gaga's Night as Jo Calderone: Was It Too Much?" *Music Mix*. Posted August 29, 2011. Retrieved August 29,

2011. http://music-mix.ew.com/2011/08/29/vmas-lady-gaga-jo-calderone/?iid=blogTMM-3H-LN-Lady%20Gaga%27s%20night%20as%20Jo%20Calderone:%20Was%20it%20too%20much?.

12. Franich, Darren. "VMAs 2011: The Winners, the Losers, and Lady Gaga." *Popwatch*. Posted August 29, 2011. Retrieved August 29, 2011. http://popwatch.ew.com/2011/08/29/mtv-vmas-2011-winners-losers/.

13. Stransky, Tanner. "MTV 2011 VMAs: Lady Gaga Explains Alter Ego Jo Calderone as a New Jersey Italian Who's 'Not a F—ing Guido!'" *Music Mix*. Posted August 29, 2011. Retrieved August 29, 2011. http://music-mix.ew.com/2011/08/28/lady-gaga-joe-calderone/.

14. Jepfan. "Yoel Brach Productions Plays L.G. Fanfare (Shaya and Perry's Wedding Intro)." *YouTube*. Posted March 17, 2010. Retrieved March 17, 2011. http://www.youtube.com/watch?v=IEiXdOOTaFs&feature=player_embedded.

15. Spuhler, Robert. "How to Make a . . . Lady Gaga." *AM NewYork*. Posted February 21, 2011. Retrieved February 21, 2011. http://www.amny.com/urbanite-1.812039/how-to-make-a-lady-gaga-1.2703839.

16. Kasparian, Anna, and Cenk Uygur. "Lady Gaga in Egg, on Pot." *The Young Turks*. Posted February 14, 2011. Retrieved March 13, 2011. http://www.youtube.com/watch?v=35XEiJBpyzM&feature=fvst.

17. Pearson, "Could You Pull off a Gaga-style Stunt?"

Chapter 6

FASHION: TURN TO THE LEFT

"What is fashion for me? Well, fashion is my lifestyle," Gaga said in an interview with 8TV, a private television station in Malaysia. "It's not dress-up, it's not a costume, it's not for show or a character. Fashion is my whole life. I've been dressing like this for maybe five or six years," she said at 25. "And when I say like this, I mean haute couture all the time. I just really found out with expressing myself through clothing, living in New York, because I wanted to make a name for myself as a musician, and it was a way for me to stand out. When I walk down the street, people said, 'I don't know who she is, but I want to know who she is.'"[1]

MADE UP OUT OF WHOLE CLOTH

The fabulous costumes that Lady Gaga wears don't appear out of thin air. A top priority for the *Haus of Gaga* is keeping up the elaborate stream of costumes. "I spend all my money on wardrobe and props. I don't care about money," Gaga is quoted as saying. "I design, I hand-make, I borrow—whatever it takes."[2]

According to *Vanity Fair*, her accessories include "Everything from crucifixes to the kitchen sink—but so far no codpiece."[3] An attentive viewer can tell that Gaga's design team re-uses garments and accessories liberally, in a mix-and-match creation of new outfits for daily wear. Several of the outfits that Gaga has worn in personal appearances at restaurants and events have appeared in her videos and are used as onstage costumes.

"My outfits get inspired by very specific things," said Gaga when pressed for details. "Sometimes from things from modern collections. Sometimes by things from the '70s or '80s. Other times I just have a vision. I can see the color and the fabric, the silhouette and all that, and I call up Dada and I say, 'I want you to make me this.'"[4]

"The singer has spent the better part of two years crafting an eccentric public persona," wrote journalist Simon Cable. "Speaking about her avant-garde image, Lady Gaga admits in the interview: 'When I wake up in the morning, I feel just like any other insecure 24-year-old girl, then I say, . . . you're Lady Gaga, you get up and walk the walk today'. "[5]

PERFORMANCE EXTREMES

In December 2009, Gaga performed on a stage built in a former synagogue in the Lower East Side of Manhattan. What used to be a Jewish immigrant tenement neighborhood was now a private concert setting for an episode of the television series *Gossip Girl*. And the plotline of the episode was that Gaga was the star performer at this private concert. The idea wouldn't have been totally implausible back when Stefani Germanotta attended Tisch School of the Arts in 2003. But college mixers are no longer a plausible performance venue for Gaga since she became an international sensation.

The red dress Gaga wore for this performance was sheer lace, with a train 16 feet long. It took three backup dancers to help her manage the train as they moved in their choreographed awkward dance. With the dancers' assistance, Gaga stepped onto a pedestal. The dancers rotated the stand, wrapping the long skirt of the dress around her feet and platform shoes. The lacy fabric looked like seafoam, but blood red. The demure pose she took made the image complete. She was meant to invoke Venus, rising from the waves in Botticelli's classic painting and David LaChapelle's photography, as Gaga later explained to a reporter from *ELLE* magazine.

By 2011, "[t]here would be almost as many costume changes as there were songs," in her concerts, according to reporters. One song began "with Gaga dressed as a nun riding the subway in lingerie humping madly on 'Love Game', switching gears to work up a frenzy on 'Boys, Boys, Boys' and 'Money Honey' before stripping off the trench coat, revealing a tiny patent-leather-look bikini, her default outfit for the two-hour show, to sing her hit single 'Telephone.'"[6]

MEAT DRESS

What's the single most provocative costume, outfit, or clothing that Gaga has worn to date? Hands down, it's the meat dress. She's worn two versions of the dress in public—one for the 2010 MTV Video Music Awards and one for a photo session with *Vogue Japan*. Just seeing a photograph of this young woman draped in flank steak is enough to cause a sensation. The People for the Ethical Treatment of Animals (PETA) condemned the outfit, referring to it as "flesh from a tortured animal."[7]

"What's everyone's big problem with my meat dress?" asked Gaga during a performance in Philadelphia in the fall of 2010. "Haven't they seen me wear leather? Next time, I'll wear a tofu dress and the soy milk police will come after me."[8]

The joke is on her, though. There really is clothing made from soybeans. The cloth is made from protein fibers left over from making tofu and other soy products. "Sometimes called vegetarian cashmere, . . . soy fibers are degradable, machine washable, resistant to bacteria and UV rays and super soft," explained a staff writer for *Vegetarian Star*. "Many soy fashions are blended with cotton and other materials."[9] Just looking at the fabric doesn't tell any passersby that the clothing was made from soybeans. There'd have to be an announcement and a press conference and a hot link from Gaga's website to the manufacturer's product descriptions online . . . which sounds pretty much like an opportunity for Gaga, if she ever has an idle moment someday.

COVER GIRL

When Gaga appeared on the cover of *Vogue* magazine, the response was generally positive. "What I love most is that Wintour and Co. didn't sanitize Gaga much at all: they put some *Vogue* polish on, but for the most part Gaga just looks like the high fashion weirdo we want her to be," said Ashley Cardiff for *The Gloss* website.[10]

On her website, Gaga is credited on the bio page with citing "rock star girlfriends, Peggy Bundy, and Donatella Versace as her fashion icons. 'I look at those artists as icons in art. It's not just about the music. It's about the performance, the attitude, the look; it's everything. And, that is where I live as an artist and that is what I want to accomplish.'"

"[E]ven when Gaga is wearing something deliberately provocative, there's always something else going on with her outfit," observed biographer Lizzy Goodman. "Maybe she's showing her breasts, but they're only visible beneath a formless blood-colored lace body sock. Or she's wearing a leotard so tight that it reveals the shape of her vagina in a grotesque way. The singer likes to exaggerate or mutate what's traditionally considered sexually provocative to the point of obscenity and revulsion. And this is what designers love about her."[11]

At the CFDA Awards, Gaga made it clear that she didn't always have access to *haute couture*. As a reporter for *New York Fashion* observed, Gaga started out in "her humble beginnings, when she wasn't rich and had to save up for her Mugler pieces."[12] Only in the fashion press could it possibly be said that starting a career in New York with the financial security of successful parents was anyone's idea of humble beginnings.

SET UP THIS WAY

The list of names in the credits goes on and on for all the creative minds responsible for the "Born This Way" video. Wigs were created by Frederic Aspiris. The nail art is credited to Aya Fukuda for Hair Room Service. During the video, Gaga wears a variety of outfits and is made up differently for each costume. She matches gloves by Portolano with a dress by Sorcha O'Raghallaigh. In various scenes, she wears knife shoes by Thierry Mugler, Natacha Marro, or shoes by Kobi Levi with a body suit designed by Atsuko Kudo. Thierry Mugler also designed technical chiffon garments. The stained glass dress was designed by Petra Storrs.

A number of designers created her accessories for the video. There was a diamond neckpiece and finger rings by Erickson Beamon, as well as a head accessory by Alexis Bittar, and earrings by Pamela Love. Nicola Formichetti worked as fashion director for this and other projects, and the imprint of his taste is visible throughout this video in particular.

The look created by all this preparation had to work as Gaga and her dancers moved in their choreographed patterns. "I thought about street kids doing alley modern dance," said Gaga, in a reference to the Ailey Modern Dance studied by her choreographer Laurieann Gibson. "The most exciting thing about the 'Born This Way' video is when we did the makeup with myself and Rico with the pink hair and matching suits," explained Gaga during an *eTalk* prime-time special in 2011. While they were setting up that scene for the video, she looked around her at the makeup and suits and told her team: "This is helium balloons away from what anyone else is doing."

REGALIA

When Anderson Cooper interviewed Gaga on *60 Minutes*, he made a reference to the performer appearing for their meeting dressed in all her regalia. "Regalia—that's a fabulous word," said Gaga instantly. "Can I steal that?" It seemed apparent that she was learning a new word. Her youth and inexperience were obvious at that moment. It takes moments like these to make it clear that this grown young woman spent her teenage years working on her performance skills. There's a wide world of knowledge out there, with which she has barely any experience. "I'm a true academic when it comes to music and my style, my fashion," said Gaga to Cooper. "There's always some sort of a story or a concept that I'm telling."

It's rare for Gaga to openly admit to stealing the words and ideas that she borrows and uses and is influenced by so freely. And regalia is pretty much exactly the word to use for the clothing Gaga wears in public. Her clothing is nearly always a careful presentation of garments that aren't ordinary or functional. The goal is to put together an outfit to present a planned appearance before an audience. Her outfits are regalia in much the same way that a priest's robe and stole are regalia. But the outfits aren't always precious and lasting like a monarch's crown and scepter. Much of what she wears when out in public and between performances looks like an improvised collage of whatever garments she had available.

Of course, her closets and suitcases always hold more than a few samples from various designers. These improvised outfits include valuable garments as well as simple flesh-tone underwear. Fans and *fashionistas* make a point of crowing on their websites about recognizing one of Gaga's garments or accessories. In January of 2009, a fashion magazine spotted her wearing vintage Versace 676 sunglasses.[13] It doesn't matter whether her audience is a television program watchers, a stadium filled to capacity with cheering fans, or a few passersby in an airport. Gaga is always dressed in her regalia of the day, ornamented in clothes meant to draw the attention of all who see her.

ARMANI

The outfit that Gaga wore on the red carpet at the Grammys in January 2010 was an Armani gown with sparkling hoops, over a sheer body stocking with long sleeves and stockings decked with rhinestones to match her shoes with platform soles and wedge heels.

In September 2010, Lady Gaga and the designer Giorgio Armani announced a multimillion dollar partnership, even though she had not met the designer in person. Few details of the deal were announced, except that Giorgio Armani would be designing costumes for Gaga's next tour.

Armani does not design ensembles meant for a specific person, even famous Hollywood actresses. But for Gaga, he has created exclusive looks that she has worn in her music video for "Alejandro," on *American Idol,* and at awards ceremonies including the Grammys and the MTV Video Music Awards. "It wouldn't be possible to give Gaga a look from the collection because she wears pieces of art," said Roberta Armani, the niece of the designer. "It's theatrical."[14]

THE FORMIDABLE NICOLA FORMICHETTI

It's hard to be sure exactly how many people participate in the artistic collective called *The Haus of Gaga.* But one of the stylists is Nicola

Formichetti. He's half-Japanese and half-Italian. The designer of Gaga's meat dress, Formichetti has become her friend as well as her stylist. Formichetti is also a fashion director with the magazine *Vogue Hommes Japan*.

At 33, Formichetti was tapped by the fashion house Thierry Mugler to be its new creative director for women's and menswear labels, overseeing their head designers. "We were looking for a young talent who could really bring new energy to the brand," said Joel Palix, the director general for Thierry Mugler.[15] The Paris-based fashion label released a statement in November 2010 that Formichetti's first collections would be for the fall–winter 2011–12 season.

Though nervous at her first fashion show, Gaga managed "to strut like a pro to her forthcoming new single Government Hooker," joining "supermodels including Jessica Stam, Coco Rocha and Alek Wek on the runway, all dressed as Gaga-alikes with flowing peroxide ponytails or white-blonde devil horns, lip-synching to the music," wrote a couple of *fashionistas* for an online version of the *Daily Mail*. "But unlike the other girls, Gaga seemed at ease walking in the towering platform shoes—an art she has mastered in her high-octane stage routines."[16] She closed the show in a distorted bridal outfit.

After the Paris show, Gaga and her entourage were a sensation at Maxim's. There's a strict dress code at this very formal restaurant. During the 1970s, actress Brigitte Bardot had created a scandal by entering the restaurant barefoot. Staid manners were to be expected at Maxim's, but Gaga did not meet that expectation.

Instead, Gaga arrived wearing a see-through leopard-print bodysuit over flesh-colored panties. On other occasions, she's worn sheer garments over similar flesh-colored underwear. Performing and crowd surfing at Lollapalooza in 2011, she wore an improvised sheer body stocking over high-rise panties as pale as her skin.

Compared with the onstage costumes of punk rock star Wendy O. Williams, the underwear seems almost prudish. There's definitely a tone that says Gaga is going just so far, but no farther. By contrast, rocker Wendy O. Williams often performed wearing only a layer of shaving cream and sometimes sheer pantyhose or a G-string. After being charged in Cleveland for obscenity, Williams took to adding a narrow strip of electrical tape on each nipple as pasties before applying the shaving cream. Starting in 1978, the "Queen of Shock Rock"[17] toured for 10 years with her band The Plasmatics. Their stage shows were punctuated by chain-sawing guitars and detonating speakers. Williams's artfully shredded offstage clothing earned her a spot among *People* magazine's Best Dressed.[18]

MAKING THE LIST

The 2010 Best Dressed List from *Vanity Fair* magazine included Lady Gaga in their originals category, along with the Duchess of Alba and fashion designer John Galliano. Gaga is listed as channeling "Gypsy Rose Elle, Salvador Dali, Isabella Blow, Caryathis, Anita Berber, and Rosie the Jetson's Robot Maid (sometimes all in one outfit)."[19] Most of the other honorees are shown in one or two photos. For Gaga, *Vanity Fair*'s photo editor selected three images. One image shows Gaga in London wearing a Jeffrey Bryant ensemble, complete with black lace mask. Another shows her "in a Philip Treacy mask at the 2010 Brit Awards,"[20] worn with a sheer body stocking by Alexander McQueen detailed with handmade lace flowers. The largest of the three photos has Gaga in one of the six outfits she wore at the Grammys in 2010, a prismatic Armani Privé blazer and crystalline crown. Under her seat is the program for the awards ceremony, and she is holding a bone china teacup. The impractical geometric lines of her showy costume contrast perfectly with the rounded curves of the teacup and saucer.

"It's not just about finding pictures of people wearing beautiful clothes," said senior photo-research editor Ann Schneider. "I seek images with life and movement that show our subjects out in the world influencing how people see things."[21] That influence is why Gaga wears her astonishing outfits on ordinary days as well as for performances and awards ceremonies. Every day is an opportunity to interact with the public and her fans, giving them something to see.

Most people never have access to clothing or costumes from fashion designers. It's safe to say that the majority of Gaga's little monsters who handmake their own versions of her costumes can't afford anything like the originals. But anyone with as little as US$30 can buy a teacup exactly like the one *Vanity Fair* shows in the photo of Gaga at the Grammys. The pattern is "Old Country Rose"—for decades the most popular pattern ever made by the Royal Albert china company. Some of Gaga's fans have their own similar teacups, bought in fine department stores, from online vendors, or in antiques shops. It's worth wondering how many of her fans found their own teacups just like Mother Monster's on a shelf in their own mother's or grandmother's kitchen.

IT'S IN THE BAG

Some women and girls will scrimp and save, or haunt sales, in order to buy an exclusive or fashionable purse. "To own a Hermès Birkin is every little girl's dream," wrote Jerico Tracy for *Harper's Magazine*. "In order to obtain one, there's a long, exclusive wait list and a hefty price tag—which is perhaps why it's the most sought-after fashion accessory in the world."[22]

While there are women who crave designer handbags, an expensive purse is not one of the things that Gaga covets. "I hate all purses," she told journalist Lisa Robinson. "I used to buy cheap, punk-looking, sloppy bags in New York, and I would stud them with stuff. I had a glue gun, and I used to glue rhinestone studs, sequins, mirrors. The disco bra from the 'Just Dance' video I made with my own two hands."[23]

It was her creative director who told Gaga she had to start carrying a practical and sensible purse. "You must buy a Birkin because it's the most classic bag,"[24] Matt Williams told her. So she did. It's a practical way to carry a bottle of water, sunglasses, and other items she might need at a moment's notice. But after carrying the simple tote bag with her as she rushed from place to place, Gaga started seeing comments on the Internet about her getting onto a private plane, holding a Hermès Birkin. Ooooh, lala, it sure didn't *look* like she hated money, wrote some *fashionista* commentators.

"So here is the irony: the most classic and iconic bag on the planet, but my fans don't relate to it because it represents something that they don't have," Gaga realized. One of the important elements in Gaga's artistic sense is a connection with her fans. "So how do I create and make it into something that they will love and adore, and turn it into a performance-art piece in itself? My fans are more iconic than this purse. I love fashion, but I don't love it more than my fans. And that's what this bag is all about."[25]

The white bag isn't in mint condition anymore. While on tour in Japan, Gaga picked up a felt pen and wrote on the white leather. In the Japanese phonetic katakana writing system, she wrote *I love little monster* and *Tokyo love*. Later during the tour, she asked Japanese artist Terence Koh to write on the purse as well. The resulting graffiti looks highly individual when the purse appears in news photographs. "Though many in the fashion world see it as the most horrific of crimes, others view it as avant-garde behavior," comments Jerico Tracy. "The bag, now covered in Japanese characters . . . has perhaps, ironically, become even more valuable."[26]

A few months of carrying a purse at odd moments seems to have mellowed Gaga's attitude about purses. She's been seen holding a second Hermès Birkin, this one black. At her request, the bag was customized with silver-tone black spike studs. The result looks anything but matronly!

WALKING A MILE IN GAGA'S SHOES

Can it be possible to wear the shoes that Gaga is seen in, day after day? Those sky-high shoes and boots bring the petite performer up to adult height. Without them, she would never be at eye level with most of the people she meets. Her shoes and boots teeter on needle-thin heels, wedge heels, and sometimes no heels at all on a stilt-like platform base. The designer Christian Louboutin had a pair of spike heels with platform soles custom-made for Gaga in black velvet in 2011. Photos show her wearing them not just with black tights, but also little white ankle socks and gold-tone chain wrapped around her ankles. "You can take the girl out of Catholic school," Gaga quipped on her blog, "but you can't take her socks."[27]

Gaga makes a particular point of wearing high-heeled shoes at all times, even when she's stepping out for a quick cup of coffee. In interviews, Gaga says that she has a horror of letting down her fans by being photographed in sloppy sweatpants and flip-flops. It's possible that she might also have a dislike for being seen as small.

The fashion statement always to be seen in heels doesn't always pay off. Instead of dressing comfortably for a transatlantic flight in June 2010, Gaga arrived at London's Heathrow airport wearing black leather chaps with a train and platform boots without heels. "However, to her shame, the singer—who prides herself on her cutting edge and outrageous fashions made by her very own design team, *Haus of Gaga*—came crashing down as she lost her balance on the ridiculous boots," wrote Simon Cable for London's *Daily News Online*. "These boots . . . were most certainly not made for walking."[28]

The heel-less platform-soled black boots that Gaga wore that day in London were designed by Noritaka Tatehana as his college graduation project. At 25, this Japanese designer was already seeing his footwear in fashion shows on Paris runways. At the request of *Style List* online magazine, he sent a similar pair of footwear in sparkly pink to their fashion department.

Fashion editor Diane Davis took on the shoe challenge. In a Cinderella moment, the shoes were tried on by most of the women in the offices where she works. Davis's feet were just the right size. At just over five feet tall, she is similar in height to Lady Gaga. With her weight thrown forward, Davis took small and careful steps. "Despite my unsteady gait, I have to say I loved being a full 10 inches taller," said Davis. "In these shoes, I felt long, lithe, and a little more authoritative as I towered over the mere mortals who assembled to cheer me on (or maybe they were waiting to see if I fell). My boss pointed out that my proportions looked entirely different and that I looked—yes!—much thinner."[29]

For much of a business day, Davis wore the shoes as she went to meetings, did presentations, and met with her colleagues in their offices. Even though Davis is used to wearing ordinary heeled pumps, the stance and gait necessary to walk in these platform shoes were so different that she kept a spotter with her at all times, particularly on the stairs. If her goal was to look thinner and taller, Davis admitted that "maybe it would be wiser to invest the $6,500 shoe price in more Pilates classes."[30]

In the opinion of a podiatrist, these shoes won't cause permanent foot damage if worn for an hour or so at a time. "Pay attention to your feet," says Dr. James Christina, director of scientific affairs for the American Podiatric Medical Association. "Our bodies are designed pretty well. When there is something that hurts, there is a reason that hurts."[31] It's worth noting that in addition to the ankle-breaker stilts,

Gaga does own comfortable pairs of sneakers for working out on her exercise machines while she's on tour.

FASHION EDITORS SPEAK THEIR MINDS

It's apparent that Lady Gaga does not present an unchanging image when she goes onstage. Even on ordinary days, when she leaves the house for her own personal errands, Gaga dresses to be seen in a variety of designer clothes and handmade garments and accessories. There is no one signature style that Gaga wears, unless her signature is looking as different as possible even when wearing pieces from outfits worn on other days and onstage. The result of this barrage of contrasting images is a delight for the paparazzi. Photographers from print and online media always have a reason to photograph Lady Gaga no matter where she is going or what she is doing. Fashion editors, however, are not always delighted with Gaga's fashion statements.

"Inasmuch as fashion is a barometer for what goes on in culture, there is a . . . tendency towards whatever is shocking," wrote fashion editor Adrien Field for the *Huffington Post*. "People at large are so jaded by vulgarity that designers, stylists, and photographers have to think of new, more perverse ways to capture people's attention. Is there any better example than the revolting circus Lady Gaga's stylist, Nicola Formichetti, sent down the runway at Thierry Mugler with tattooed goblins?"[32]

The Lady Gaga media phenomenon seems to be an opportunity for some writers to express extravagantly negative opinions. A Canadian music reviewer commented in 2011 on one of Gaga's Toronto shows beginning "90 minutes late, a delay long enough to weary even the Gaga imitators strutting about with skulls painted on their faces, yellow caution tape wrapped around their bodies, and no pants."[33] Perhaps the theatrical, showy style of Gaga's arrivals and performances invites reviewers to use a similarly high-strung mode of expression. Certainly that writer had no snide comments in print about fans lounging around in long hair and blue jeans at a Neil Young concert in Toronto.

Gaga is described as "a fame whore who gains extra attention by wearing ridiculous clothing befitting characters from a bad science fiction novel," according to media website commentator Scott Tunstall. He goes on to add, "One day, hopefully soon, her act will wear thin. But until such time we can look forward to more Lady Gaga dressed like an idiot from outer space."[34]

CATTY COMMENTS ONLINE

Fashion commentators have taken to using the name of Lady Gaga as shorthand for describing a fashion statement that is not only unique but overboard. A satirical essay on fashion appeared on *The Gloss* website in April 2010. "Hi bears. Are you tired of looking frumpy after hibernating all winter?" asked writer Allie Brosh. "Maybe you are looking to add a little spark to your wardrobe but you are afraid of going overboard and looking like a furry Lady Gaga / yak hybrid covered in deer blood."[35] Brosh's talent as a comic strip writer led her to produce this series of sketches and fashion advice for grizzly bears. Her humor actually made some sense of the Lady Gaga reference, from blood smears, defining your waist, and choosing accessories carefully.

"It's not every day that I would wear something that Lady Gaga also wore," wrote another writer for *The Gloss*. "I'm not super flashy in the way I dress . . . and I don't usually wear costumes on, say, any old Wednesday. But I would totally rock these sunglasses, and I would rock them hard, because I live in L.A.,"[36] she states, speaking of a pair of round, brown lenses with bronze frames.

Gaga's beachwear was the topic of another brief article for *The Gloss*. "Lady Gaga, spotted here vacationing with her boyfriend Lüc Carl on the Greek island of Crete, wore a metal bikini to sun herself," wrote Ashley Cardiff in October 2010. "Maybe Gaga just never turns off or maybe she's trying to get some extra wear out of a reliably excellent Halloween costume."[37]

These opinions may be more than a little catty, but they're not really cruel. In particular, the writers are making statements that are fair comments. Gaga's fashion choices are intended to provoke discussion and thought. Some of her choices are more obvious than others. A good example of that obviousness was the choice by then-teenaged Stefani Germanotta to strip down to her underwear when performing in front of inattentive nightclub crowds.

"A lot of the appeal of sexiness is that it's really, really obvious. You don't have to think very hard about why a schoolgirl stripping naked might be sexually appealing to people," wrote Jennifer Wright for *The Gloss*. "To be truly sexy, your outfit should communicate only one thing. 'I like sex! I like it any way you want it! And you totally have a chance with me!' Lady Gaga's outfits keep communicating things about, say, the nature of modern warfare and lobsters. This is, perhaps, sexy, but only to Salvador Dali."[38]

The Gloss website has had a lot to say about Gaga over the last couple of years. The length of time the writers have made such remarks is itself a comment on the performer's longevity. She is no flash in the pan. Gaga's career has lasted longer than many online publications. For this performer, there is no such thing as bad publicity.

GAGA AND QUEEN ELIZABETH

Some of Gaga's costumes have a clear message behind the weird images. Perhaps her most meaningful costume so far was one that she wore in December 2009 for her performance for Queen Elizabeth II of England. It was a dress that covered her from neck to wrists and ankles. It wasn't transparent or torn or smudged with ashes. But it was hardly modest.

Her dress for that Royal performance was "a painted-on lipstick red latex S&M gown, featuring a twenty-foot train and a high, tight collar that looked as if it could actually choke her," wrote fashion commentator Lizzy Goodman. In her opinion, the pop singer was like "a satanic version of Elizabeth I." This historical figure was not only a namesake for the current Queen, but a powerful symbol of female strength in government. Dressing in a style anything like a Tudor gown, particularly when performing in front of the Queen of England, was an artistic statement: Lady Gaga is like Elizabeth the First. "Famous for her refusal to marry, the so-called Virgin Queen considered courtship to be a political tactic. She weighed every decision about sexuality and relationships against what would be good for her country, and she concluded that marriage would only weaken her political power. So she stayed single for life, referring to her English subjects as 'all my husbands, my good people.' As a result, her people vaulted her to saintlike status."[39]

Gaga prepared carefully for this performance. She rejected her first idea, about bleeding on stage, as too extreme for her royal audience. It seemed more moderate to play keyboards at a piano elevated above the stage. As well, she practiced how to curtsy, which is not easy to do in high heels and a dress with a train. Instead, when introduced to the Queen, Gaga bobbed in more of a bow than a formal curtsy.

DRESSED LIKE A QUEEN

Several of Lady Gaga's fantasy gowns are the product of the studio of Alexander McQueen. The head of the studio, McQueen, was known to friends by his first name, Lee. When he committed suicide at 40 on February 11, 2010, the studio was deeply affected. Many of the designs McQueen made for Gaga remain in her wardrobe. His right-hand associate, Sarah Burton, worked with him for a dozen years before taking over the management of the studio. "Burton was confirmed as the creative director of Alexander McQueen, part of the Gucci Group, in May last year [2010, after McQueen's suicide]," noted a fashion reviewer. "She has also created one-off designs for Cate Blanchett, Lady Gaga, and Gwyneth Paltrow."[40] As well as designing collections in 2011, Burton created a red-and-black billowing dress for Michelle Obama to wear at a state dinner.

Burton usually avoids being photographed. The few images of her in public show her usually wearing flat-soled ballet pumps and a distinctive silver-link belt. Jeans and a blouse don't look sloppy with the right accessories. That's something Gaga herself knew back in her student days at Tisch, wearing suspenders on her jeans.

The Gucci Group designers have dressed Gaga like royalty for her red carpet walks at awards events. They have dressed her to meet the Queen of England. And in a crowning royal touch, Sarah Burton designed the wedding dress worn by Catherine Middleton to marry Prince William in April 2011.

There was only one particular similarity between that traditional wedding gown and the costumes Burton and her colleagues have made for Gaga. It is an important similarity. Handmade lace flowers appear on several of Gaga's garments, and on the bodice and sleeves of Middleton's wedding dress. These bits of lace have been individually placed onto the background material of *point d'esprit* lace.

The time-consuming work of hand-sewing each lace flower is worth the effort. The garment drapes well when the stiffened lace is placed properly. It flatters the particular shape of the woman who is being adorned. It is worth noticing that the designer and seamstresses made costumes for Lady Gaga showing the same attention and skill as in the gown they made for the Royal Wedding. They dressed Gaga like they dressed the woman who one day will be Queen of England.

WORKING CLOTHES

Even when she's not trying to be outrageous, Gaga's fashion choices when attending public events are intended to get her attention. Passersby and onlookers do double-takes when Gaga arrives. One of her more straightforward outfits in 2011 matched large black sunglasses, black tights, and purse with a little wraparound leopard-print robe that her mother picked up at JC Penney.

Another classic—the little black dress—got updated when Gaga went to La Maison De Fashion one August night in 2011. When she left the Los Angeles store in the wee hours of the morning, fans and paparazzi spotted her dressed up—or down—for the occasion in a short black sheath. As *OK!* magazine quipped: "We are so used to seeing Gaga in crazy outfits and barely-there attire, she stunned the cameras with her little black dress that she looked flawless in!"[41]

Of course, this Versace version of a little black dress included one shoulder, a slit to the hip, oversized gold buttons, and a large floral swirl. Her manicure showed off lethally long nails painted red as the soles of her spike-heeled Louboutin pumps. Summer weather made this a good time to wear her dark sunglasses with a long, smooth hairstyle. And the woman who hates purses held a little black clutch in one hand. "Maybe she's got tired of her crazy costumes and tried out this girly look,"[42] commented one website for fashion fans.

It seems that everything Gaga is ever seen wearing is a necessary part of her presentation. Some of the black bikinis she wears onstage are as simple and practical as the swimsuits she wore on a beach in Mexico in August 2011, when learning to ride a surfboard. And yes, she took off her high heels and slipped on little neoprene shoes that gripped the board when she stood to ride the waves. The same style of black, brief swimsuits she has performed in so many times looked even more practical and powerful in the surf.

"You must desire the reality of fantasy so profusely that it becomes necessity, not *accessory*,"[43] Gaga wrote for V *Magazine*. But it's when she puts her accessories to their proper use that she creates the greatest images of strength.

At a protest rally in Portland, Maine, in 2010, she wore a mannish black suit with white shirt and polka-dot necktie. Before she spoke out in favor of repealing the "Don't Ask, Don't Tell" legislation, Gaga pushed up her sleeves and pushed back the waves of her yellow hair. It was time to go to work, said her manner. Her suit reinforced that message.

NOTES

1. LadyGagaBeforeM. "Lady Gaga Interview 8TV Quickie Malaysia." *8TV Quickie*. Posted February 10, 2011. Retrieved March 24, 2011. http://wn.com/8TV_Quickie.

2. Pop Style. "Lady Gaga: 18 Outrageous Outfits." *Entertainment Weekly*. Posted February 4, 2010. Retrieved April 20, 2011. http://www.ew.com/ew/gallery/0,,20309550_20309885,00.html#20635417.

3. Schneider, Ann. "2010 Best Dressed List." *Vanity Fair*. September 2010, p. 244.

4. LadyGagaBeforeM, "Lady Gaga Interview 8TV Quickie Malaysia."

5. Cable, Simon. "Well It Was Bound to Happen . . . Lady Gaga Takes a Tumble Thanks to Her Ridiculous Choice of Footwear." *The Daily Mail Online*. Posted June 24, 2011. Retrieved March 4, 2011. http://www.dailymail.co.uk/tvshowbiz/article-1288980/Lady-Gaga-takes-tumble-thanks-ridiculous-choice-footwear.html.

6. Armstrong, Denis. "Concert Review: Lady Gaga Scotiabank Place, Ottawa—March 7, 2011." *Jam*. Posted March 8, 2011. Retrieved March 13, 2011. http://jam.canoe.ca/Music/Artists/L/Lady_GaGa/ConcertReviews/2011/03/08/17532381.html.

7. Metro Lyrics. "Lady Gaga Laughs Off Meat Dress Criticism." *Metro Lyrics*. Posted September 19, 2010. Retrieved March 24, 2011. http://www.metrolyrics.com/2010-lady-gaga-laughs-off-meat-dress-criticism-news.html.

8. Vegetarian Star. "Lady Gaga Threatening to Wear Soy Now. Call Her Bluff!" *Vegetarian Star.* Posted October 1, 2010. Retrieved March 24, 2011. http://vegetarianstar.com/2010/10/01/lady-gaga-threatening-to-wear-soy-now-call-her-bluff/.

9. Ibid.

10. Cardiff, Ashley. "Under Cover: Lady Gaga's American 'Vogue' Is Here." *The Gloss.* Posted February 10, 2011. Retrieved March 16, 2011. http://thegloss.com/fashion/under-cover-lady-gagas-american-vogue-is-here/.

11. Goodman, Lizzy. "Revulsion as Fashion." *Lady Gaga: Critical Mass Fashion.* New York: St. Martin's Press, 2010, p. 136.

12. Odell, Amy. "Lady Gaga on Texting Anna Wintour, Anderson Cooper on Child Modeling, and More Highlights from the CFDA Awards." *New York Fashion.* Posted June 7, 2011. Retrieved June 7, 2011. http://nymag.com/daily/fashion/2011/06/lady_gaga_on_texting_anna_wint.html.

13. Croteau, Lauren. "Lady Gaga Wearing Vintage Versace Sunglasses." *The Gloss.* Posted January 18, 2009. Retrieved March 17, 2011. http://thegloss.com/fashion/lady-gaga-wearing-vintage-versace-sunglasses-2–685/?utm_source=splendicity&utm_medium=web&utm_campaign=b5hubs_migration. Page no longer available.

14. "Lady Gaga & Armani Strike Multimillion Dollar Deal." *The Huffington Post.* Posted September 27, 2010. Retrieved March 4, 2011. http://www.huffingtonpost.com/2010/09/27/lady-gaga-armani-deal_n_740774.html.

15. AP. "Nicola Formichetti Appointed Creative Director of Thierry Mugler." *The Huffington Post.* Posted November 14, 2010. Retrieved March 4, 2011. http://www.huffingtonpost.com/2010/09/14/nicola-formichetti-appoin_n_715860.html.

16. Thompson, Jody, and Tamara Abraham. "What Dress Code? Lady Gaga Dons See-Through Leopard Print Catsuit for Dinner at Paris's Fancy Restaurant Maxim's." *The Daily Mail Online.* Posted March 3, 2011. Retrieved March 4, 2011. http://www.dailymail.co.uk/tvshowbiz/article-1362479/Lady-Gaga-leopard-print-catsuit-Paris-restaurant-Maxims.html.

17. API. "Punk Singer Wendy O. Williams Dies." *Wendy O. William's Death.* Posted 1998. Retrieved March 5, 2011. http://www.modernatomic.com/plasmatics/wendysdead.html.

18. Rush, Charles. "Style Stars of '81." *People Magazine*, Vol. 16 # 12. September 21, 1981, p. 34. http://www.people.com/people/archive/article/0,,20080256,00.html.

19. Schneider, Ann. "2010 Best Dressed List." *Vanity Fair*. September 2010, p. 244.

20. Ibid.

21. Schneider, Ann. "Contributors." *Vanity Fair*. September 2010, p. 140.

22. Tracy, Jerico. "Gaga Revises Birkin." *Harper's Bazaar*. Posted April 21, 2010. Retrieved May 24, 2011. http://www.harpersbazaar.com.au/gaga-revises-birkin.htm.

23. Robinson, Lisa. "Lady Gaga's Cultural Revolution." *Vanity Fair*. September 2010, p. 280.

24. Ibid.

25. Ibid.

26. Tracy, "Gaga Revises Birkin."

27. Lady Gaga. *Amen Fashion*. Posted July, 2011. Retrieved August 10, 2011. http://amenfashion.tumblr.com/.

28. Cable, Simon. "Well It Was Bound to Happen . . . Lady Gaga Takes a Tumble Thanks to Her Ridiculous Choice of Footwear." *The Daily Mail Online*. Posted June 24, 2011. Retrieved March 4, 2011. http://www.dailymail.co.uk/tvshowbiz/article-1288980/Lady-Gaga-takes-tumble-thanks-ridiculous-choice-footwear.html.

29. Davis, Diane. "Walking in Lady Gaga's Shoes." *Style List.com*. Posted November 4, 2010. Retrieved March 4, 2011. http://www.stylelist.com/2010/11/04/lady-gaga-shoes/.

30. Ibid.

31. Ibid.

32. Field, Adrien. "Where Did the Glamour Go?" *The Huffington Post*. Posted January 21, 2011. Retrieved March 4, 2011. http://www.huffingtonpost.com/adrien-field/where-did-the-glamour-go_b_812270.html.

33. Everett-Green, Rupert. "Lurid, Bitter, Swaggering, Maternal—and Oddly Real." Globe Arts. *The Globe and Mail*. March 5, 2011, p. R2.

34. Tunstall, Scott. "15 Pics of Lady Gaga Dressed Like an Idiot." *Gunaxin Media*. Posted March 2, 2011. Retrieved April 15, 2011. http://media.gunaxin.com/15-pics-of-lady-gaga-dressed-like-an-idiot/83972?utm_source=scribol&utm_medium=referral&utm_campaign=scribol.

35. Brosh, Allie. "Allie Brosh Presents: The Grizzly Bear's Guide to Flattering Fashion." *The Gloss*. Posted April 16, 2010. Retrieved March 17, 2010. http://thegloss.com/fashion/allie-brosh-presents-the-grizzly-bears-guide-to-flattering-fashion/.

36. Ogilvie, Jessica Pauline. "I Covet Lady Gaga's Sunglasses." *The Gloss*. Posted October 22, 2010. Retrieved March 17, 2011. http://thegloss.com/fashion/i-covet-lady-gagas-sunglasses/.

37. Cardiff, Ashley. "This is What Lady Gaga Wears to the Beach." *The Gloss*. Posted October 20, 2010. Retrieved March 17, 2011. http://thegloss.com/fashion/this-is-what-lady-gaga-wears-to-the-beach/.

38. Wright, Jennifer. "Gallery: Lady Gaga Is Not 'Sexy.'" *The Gloss*. Posted August 3, 2010. Retrieved March 16, 2011. http://thegloss.com/beauty/gallery-lady-gaga-is-not-sexy/.

39. Goodman. "Revulsion as Fashion," p. 136.

40. Alexander, Hilary. "Sartorial Slip Gives Tantalizing Clue to the Most Closely Guarded Secret of Day." *Victoria Times-Colonist*. Posted April 29, 2011. Retrieved April 29, 2011. http://www.timescolonist.com/life/Sartorial+slip+gives+tantalizing+clue+most+closely+guarded+secret/4694032/story.html.

41. OK! Staff. "Lady Gaga Shows Off Her Glamorous Side in L.A." *OK!* Posted August 12, 2011. Retrieved August 14, 2011. http://www.ok-magazine.com/2011/08/lady-gaga-shows-off-her-glamorous-side-in-l-a/.

42. "Lady Gaga Looks Normal: Shocking!" *StyleBistro*. Posted August 12, 2011. Retrieved August 14, 2011. http://www.stylebistro.com/Fashion+Forum/articles/TlZGcZKfCx6/Lady+Gaga+Looks+Normal+Shocking. Page no longer available.

43. Lady Gaga. "From the Desk of Lady Gaga." *V Magazine*. Posted July 2011. Retrieved August 10, 2011. http://www.vmagazine.com/2011/07/from-the-desk-of-lady-gaga-2/.

Chapter 7

ONLINE WITH THE LITTLE MONSTERS

"Do I feel like a powerful person in show business? Yeah,"[1] said Gaga when asked by shock radio host Howard Stern if she will use her influence in the industry for good or evil.

"I'm not looking to be worshipped by the world," Gaga said in an *eTalk* prime-time special in May 2011. "I want to worship my fans. I don't want to be your queen." She went on to insist that she hated perfection. "I think that it's the flaws in myself, the flaws in the world, the flaws in my fans, that make them beautiful."

GAGAVISION

Only a few months after beginning to work with Interscope, Gaga began making short videos about her life as a working performer. These short films were uploaded weekly to her website. The project was called Transmission Gagavision. In spite of all the demands on her time, Gaga kept up her MySpace page and Facebook wall.

"She cracked a code that's ever-changing, specific to each person who tries," reported Maureen Callahan. "How to cut through the clutter of the Web and create an online presence that's not just startling but that sticks, that keeps people coming back in ever-greater numbers, and that then translates into the real world, generating actual currency—be they votes for president or tickets to your rock show."[2] The Gagavision videos paused for a while in 2010 and resumed in 2011, more effective than ever.

"With the Internet, everybody gets distribution, everybody gets eyeballed. But fame and stickiness? That depends on the content," said Tony DiSanto of MTV. "There are a million artists and a million kids out there putting stuff up on *YouTube* every day, so it's a lot easier to get seen, but it's much harder to get famous. Because with this much choice, things get lost in the middle."[3]

NEWS FLASH

Integrating her news releases with her public appearances and stage performances, Gaga not only keeps her fans informed about her activities, but she also keeps them feeling connected to her. "After winning Video of the Year for 'Bad Romance'—which capped off an evening that resulted in eight VMA awards—Lady Gaga made good on a promise to fans by revealing the title of her next album, due in 2011: *Born This Way*."[4]

One of the results of keeping her promises is that Gaga has great credibility and interest for millions of devoted fans. Books and comic books are marketed to her devotees, proclaiming: "From her early days at NYU to her music videos and MTV performances, become one of her little monsters and take a look behind the curtain to learn the truth about pop-music diva."[5] Other promotional materials ask: "Is it the costumes? The music? The voice? Maybe it's all that stage blood. Whatever the reason, Lady GaGa has become one of pop music's biggest stars." Bluewater Comics asked the rhetorical question, "Is there room for everyone in the *Haus of GaGa?*"[6] Apparently, there just might be room for everyone, from ten-year-olds to international fashion designers.

"A huge company like Giorgio Armani has the duty to always be alert to trends and what appeals to young people," said Roberta Armani, niece of designer Giorgio Armani, when Gaga and Armani announced a multimillion dollar partnership in 2010. "It helped to see how the world is through Lady Gaga, the way she uses Facebook and Twitter."[7]

ONE NIGHT AMONG MANY

Many of the concerts on the Monster Ball tour had much in common with other events along the tour. The unique element at one of these concerts was the personal experience. Unlike their globe-trotting idol, many of the little monsters don't have the resources to travel from concert to concert. For most of the young people attending her concerts, this is the first time they've seen her in person. "There was excitement and hairspray a-plenty in the air," wrote Denis Armstrong for *Jam* magazine in Ottawa, "as some 12,000 little monsters, composed largely of glamorous drag queens, glitter boys and Lady Gaga wannabes braved a late-winter blast for what might easily be the pop concert of the year."[8]

"I didn't used to be brave," Gaga said at that Ottawa concert on March 6, 2011. "In fact, I wasn't very brave at all, but you have made me brave, little monsters. Somehow, I'm going to be brave for you. Tonight I want you to forget all of your insecurities." A Canadian reviewer wrote that "Gaga shared many of her own insecurities about performing, not fitting in, being bullied and questioning Jesus. At times, she looked like a mess, her face smeared with make-up and fake blood as she let it all hang out. Set against the tightly run choreography and singing of her performance numbers, however, it made her seem human."[9]

"Life is a ball and it's always better when you're dressed up," said Ana Matronic, one of the members of Scissor Sisters, at the opening act for the Ottawa concert. "Among those who subscribed to the same notion was a group of eight mothers between the ages of 29 and 52 who said it took them three hours to don their fabulous outfits. When asked what the key elements of a Gaga costume were, they listed blond hair, sunglasses, outrageous accessories and 'lots of leg.'"

As the eight walked up to the door to the concert venue, traffic stopped—including the mayor's vehicle. "'Now I know what it's like to have paparazzi,' laughed one as other passersby snapped their shots. The moms' outing was organized by event planner Stephanie Cummings, who, over the last six months or so, gave each of her friends a ticket to the show for her birthday, and swore them to secrecy. 'We love (Gaga's) individuality, her creativity, her love of fashion, her music, her dancing,' Cummings said. 'Everything about her is so positive. It makes you feel good.' She's convinced that Gaga is an artist who will stand the test of time. 'She doesn't lip sync. She is live, she is real, she is authentic. And you know when she sings, it's coming from within her and captivating everyone around her.'"[10]

BROKEN RECORDS

It's hard to think of the Internet as having a center. That's the main reason for the way so many information servers are connected together—there is no center, no one place where every piece of information begins its journey. But there is a place that many pieces of information pass through—the headquarters for the most popular search engine on the Internet. That place is Google headquarters in California, which Lady Gaga visited in 2011.

Another information center is not on the Internet—it's a book! The *Guinness World Records* is an honorable tradition, founded in the United Kingdom by the company that makes a dark beer known round the world as "Guinness." In a stroke of marketing genius, the company began collecting into book form information about world record events. The idea was that copies of the book could be kept in bars and pubs to settle arguments and disputes.

In mid-September 2010, an announcement came from the Guinness World Records organization that the record had been broken for the singer with the most consecutive weeks on the U.K. charts. The previous record had been 134 weeks, held by Oasis. The new record was held by Lady Gaga. Since the August 2008 release of singles from *The Fame*, Lady Gaga had been in the Top 75 on the U.K. charts for 154 weeks. In the 17 years that the *Billboard* Pop Songs chart has been publishing, Gaga was the first artist to score four number one hits from one album.

Another record was broken as well, according to the 2011 edition of the *Guinness World Records*. Gaga is "now officially the Most Searched-For Female on the Internet," reported MTV's website. "Gaga takes her place alongside late pop icon Michael Jackson, the Most Searched-For Male on the Internet."[11] Internet searches for "lady gaga" outnumbered those for the previous most searched-for female: Sarah Palin, the former governor of Alaska. The *Guinness World Records* noted as well that Gaga also was the first artist to have her videos viewed more than a billion times, with three of her videos joining the 100 million club.

SPOKESWOMAN?

At the end of 2009, Gaga told the *Observer* that the high point of the year for her had been her relationship with the gay community. "My fans have a soul," she said. "They're a subculture of music lovers, pop music lovers, misfits, an incredible group of young people who all have something in common and come to my shows to be freed."[12]

But it seems that while Gaga has millions of fans, not every gay person regards her as the ideal poster girl to speak to the world for them. "Among her supposed heartland of gay men, there's growing evidence of fans starting to turn on her—many of whom feel she has no right to declare herself as the ambassador of 'queer culture,'" reported Dan Martin for the *Guardian*. He admits that Gaga didn't have to put too much effort into becoming accepted as an icon for some gays. "There's a certain mainstream gay sensibility that tends to adopt blonde female pop stars as their own, and her relentless tweeting about gay rights, the impassioned stance against Don't Ask Don't Tell in the US military, and yes, I suppose the dresses too, earned her a place as a credible advocate," he acknowledges. "But recently, the wheels seem to be falling off, and sadly not from that ridiculous motorbike. . . . But as the world lived with Born This Way, a deeper disquiet began to emerge, and the heavy-handed way that the song assumed stewardship of an entire portion of humanity began to breed real resentment, from the forums to the dancefloor to the word on the street."

As Dan Martin pointed out, the fact of the matter is that most gay people don't consider themselves freaks who are outside the cultural norms, as suggested in Lady Gaga's song lyrics. He believes that most homosexuals feel they are perfectly normal people whose sexual orientation just happens to be wired in this way. "And they won't thank you for attempting to lead a Pied Piper march back into the ghetto with all the subtlety of a diamond-encrusted sledgehammer. We're a lot closer to the dream where sexual orientation doesn't define a person, but is a quality of their personality no more or less significant than their political affiliation or the color of their hair." In the progression toward real equality, the concept of gay culture has less meaning as more people come to understand that gay people aren't all the same. "In the face of that, 'Born This Way' was at best a backward step, in the middle a touch cynical and, at worst, downright offensive," wrote Martin. "It's a shame because it was the first real misstep in an otherwise faultlessly judged career."[13]

MENTORING YOUTH

In some ways, Gaga seems very protective of her fans. She gives them advice and motivational speeches during concerts and interviews, sometimes as if speaking directly to her listeners. "To any little sweethearts that are listening," she said in an aside while being interviewed by Howard Stern, "don't touch [cocaine], it's the devil."[14]

Gaga has begun to act as a mentor for younger performers. In particular, one teenage boy who recorded his own version of one of Gaga's songs has had his life changed. He spoke with Gaga, appeared on the talk show *Ellen*, and now has a recording contract.

One of the newest members of her band is Judy Kang, the teenage violinist from Edmonton who played with Gaga on the Monster Ball tour. Kang's solos on a pink electric violin were a highlight of the tour performances in Toronto and Ottawa. "As I play, I want to be not just someone up there entertaining," Kang said during a CBC television news report on March 5, 2011, "but I want to be an instrument bringing something to the people who are there."

LADY MARIA

Days after the much-anticipated release of Gaga's single "Born This Way," a small video was also released on YouTube. It showed 10-year-old Maria Aragon singing Gaga's newest song and accompanying herself on an electronic keyboard. Maria's mother filmed the girl singing in a plain room at their home in Canada and uploaded the video to YouTube. Friends watched the recording, and some fans of Gaga found it and watched it as well. Then something special happened. News of

Maria's video went viral. In just a few days, millions of people tracked down her video, watched it, and sent the link to their friends. By the time Gaga saw it, the video was must-see news for any Gaga fan.

Seeing the girl's natural delivery of her song brought Gaga to tears. It didn't take any pressure on her part to publicize the recording. Bowing gracefully to the inevitable, Gaga was pleased to announce that at her next Canadian appearance, Maria would sing "Born This Way" with her.

Speaking of her series of interviews on *Good Morning, America,* on *Ellen,* and other shows, Maria said on a CBC news report on March 3, 2010, that it was like a domino effect and had become tiring, but it's all for people's entertainment, and it's all good. After a two-week whirlwind, the 10-year-old appeared with Lady Gaga in concert in Toronto, Ontario, Canada. She was introduced to the crowd as "Lady Maria." The roar of recognition showed that everyone there was familiar with the story of the little girl. That very morning her homemade music video had topped 17 million views on YouTube.

The costume for "Lady Maria" was both flashy and age-appropriate. In an outfit of pink-and-black pants and shirt with a white porkpie hat, Maria looked bright and energetic, yet still a child with a furry monkey Velcro-ed round her neck. The ensemble made a sensible contrast to the shiny black bikini and knee-high boots worn by Lady Gaga at that point in the night's show.

Together, Gaga and Maria sang "Born This Way" without any of the suggestive dance moves highlighted in the music video. Instead, they were simply sitting at the piano with Maria on Gaga's lap. Maria played the keys, while Gaga worked the pedals and added a little left-handed bass line. The Canadian audience was thrilled, and at the end of the concert, their cheers rose even louder when Maria returned to sing an encore with Gaga. Their songs together were the simplest parts of a show that had been well-rehearsed on tour to showcase thrilling dancing and body-reshaping costumes.

"You could say that little Maria Aragon stole this show, except that Lady Gaga handed it to her on a plate," said Rupert Everett-Green, who reviewed the concert for Toronto's *Globe and Mail* newspaper. "What could have been a mere publicity stunt—pop star invites Winnipeg 10-year-old with a video cam to sing on the Monster Ball tour—

became the most emotionally charged episode in a forceful, lurid and often bizarre concert."[15]

There were record companies wanting to sign up young Maria on the spot, and she just might take them up on the offer. But Maria's first big plan for after the concert was to return home to Winnipeg and her ordinary life.

NOT THE ONLY ONE

Text messaging has become a convenient form of communication. It's not just a way that Lady Gaga tries to foster a sense of community with her fans. It's also the way she receives a good deal of her business communications.

When Gaga learned that she had won the Fashion Icon Award from CFDA, it was from a text message. Anna Wintour wrote a brief note saying "We're so excited to tell you won the CFDA fashion icon award," and Gaga told the crowd about the note in her acceptance speech. "I actually thought it was Anna Treblin," she said at the awards event on June 7, 2011.

The reply Gaga sent was appropriate for Anna Treblin, who was Nicola Fermengetti's assistant and one of her own close friends: "Yes, bitch, we did it." Gaga admitted that quite quickly she got a reply saying, "How lovely, and we will all be waiting to see what you will wear."[16]

After a moment's thought, Gaga realized that she wasn't texting the Anna who would be helping choose what she would wear. This wasn't the buddy Anna who would be going out with her for a drink, it was Anna Wintour of CFDA. Oops!

Late on the evening of the award event, Gaga's Facebook status was updated. "A whirlwind NY night. I'm honored to receive CFDA's Fashion Icon Award. Little Monsters, we did it!"[17] She knew that a fashion icon doesn't walk alone in the world.

TWITTER NOTES

Twitter is a way through which fans can feel an instant connection to celebrities, as if they were close friends. One of the purposes Gaga has for her Twitter account is to bring ideas to the attention of her fans—

news about political activism as well as news bites about her own re-cordings and appearances. "Buffalo, we need SEN.GRISANTI to help pass NY STATE MARRIAGE BILL," she tweeted in early March, in-cluding the senator's e-mail address at the senate of New York state. She also sent updates on the bill's progress through the state legislature.

Anyone who receives Twitter updates from Lady Gaga, or reads them online, knows both her press release news and simple things such as her love for Nutella sandwiches on Wonderbread with bananas. "How Ironic, head full of bleach + two black Cruella stripes," she sent one day while her hair was being done. "Scalp burning, Mole draw-ing, eyeliner dripping. Waiting for #Hair. I could Dye."[18] Sometimes the Internet is used for nothing of world-shattering importance, just a moment of human connection between friends or family, or a celebrity and her fans. One March day, Gaga tweeted "Glass of wine + a nail file, bedtime heaven. Some things never change."[19]

In May 2011, the name of the first person to have 10 million Twitter followers was announced. To no one's surprise, it was Lady Gaga. "Can hear 30,000 Monsters slamming the stadium floor in Guadalajara," she tweeted in May. "It sounds pop revolution, fists pounding furiously."[20]

CONNECTED

These days, social media is as indispensable as the telephone, particu-larly for promoting entertainment. Over 44 million people like Gaga's fan page on Facebook. Even her sunglasses made of cigarettes—the ones that appeared in the video for "Telephone"—have their own Facebook page.

"Unquestionably, Gaga has mastered the art of using social media to promote herself, her products and her message. Her Twitter followers and her Facebook fans are not just people who listen to her music. They are her devoted fans and loyal customers—her "Little Monsters—who helped move 1 million digital downloads of her recent single 'Born This Way' in only five days," commented a writer for *Forbes* business magazine. "They're also happy to buy the MAC makeup, Monster headphones and Virgin Mobile phones she features in her videos."[21]

Gaga's BlackBerry phone is never far from her. Among other things, it holds little audio clips as she comes up with ideas that get incorporated into new songs. She also uses the BlackBerry to send Twitter notes and to update her Facebook status.

When Gaga has an idle moment, it's not really more than a moment. In the back of a limousine on the way to a gala, she might take out her phone and send a quick update. Some of these notes are promotional tidbits about her new songs being released. "FASHION OF HIS LOVE is about Alexander McQueen,"[22] was one such note. Another said "HIGHWAY UNICORN is about me. Flying down the road, with nothing but a dream."[23]

Other notes are idle filler about meeting her friends for some fun. These notes will not change the world, but they do give the reader a sense of connection with small details in an ordinary day for Gaga. There are also notes that show that she (or a trusted associate) reads some of the replies to each of her tweets and updates. One tweet said in reply to a fan's note: "I just read it. You're kick ass beautiful, don't beat yourself up. Let your identity be your religion, my religion is you. X"[24]

THE PERSONAL TOUCH

Some kinds of promotion work best in person, with face-to-face interaction. The day her album *Born This Way* was released, Lady Gaga appeared on *Late Night with David Letterman* after launching the album at a Best Buy store. Letterman seemed quite taken with her outfit: a black jacket over black bikini, worn with a mask and artistic hat, stockings, and boots. Apparently he did some research about Gaga and the music industry, because he asked if you can make money with albums. Gaga insisted that yes, you can. She has sold 24 million copies of the first two records. There are royalties coming to her.

Speaking with Letterman about how one trains for life as a pop star, Gaga talked a little about the burlesque show she used to do in New York with her friend Lady Starlight, covering heavy metal tunes. "We used to do a variety show. We would wear matching bikinis," she said, coyly. "If you take your clothes off it's amazing what will happen."

"When I was your age, I had a paper route," Letterman protested. "In my line of work, I don't know that they can teach you how to ride disco sticks." Instead, he wanted to know more about the egg that she appeared in at the Emmys. What was up with that?

"For me it is a place where I can meditate and experience rebirth," Gaga told him. "I just get inside it and close it, and when I feel I have been reborn spiritually, I just whoo!"[25] Spiritual rebirth didn't impress Letterman as much as her meat dress had.

ALTER EGO MISSTEP

"From a meat dress to a firework-producing brassiere, the pop diva's style often produces shock and awe. So no one could have predicted that a simple fish fin would incite a feud between several pop divas and cause more buzz than any outfit before. With Katy Perry and Bette Midler crying foul, the 'Born This Way' singer has got to be feeling that there are way too many fish in the sea," commented Brett Chukerman for *Yahoo!* "The icon announced a mermaid alter ego named 'Yuji' earlier this summer [2011], and was recently on stage in a wheelchair as the land-locked fish—an act made famous by Bette Midler thirty years ago."[26]

"You can keep the meat dress and the firecracker tits—mermaid's mine," Midler declared on Twitter.[27] "I've been doing singing mermaid in a wheelchair since 1980," Chukerman quotes Midler as tweeting to Gaga. He went on to say that "Though the two have seemingly made up over the issue, it certainly does not help Gaga in her constant quest of proving she is wholly original and not a copycat of artists like Midler, Madonna and Cher."[28] He noted that Madonna also wore a mermaid tail in 1989 during her video for "Cherish." Though Katy Perry wore a mermaid suit in some promotional Twitter notes, when Gaga appeared onstage later that month as a mermaid, Perry began developing another onstage persona instead.

"I had no idea that she did that and I'm a huge Bette Midler fan," Gaga finally commented to *Access Hollywood* on the "splash." Writer Sean Michaels felt that seemed "a little disingenuous" as any huge fan would be familiar with Midler playing the role of Delores Delgaso.[29]

Another Twitter response to Gaga's Yuji appearance came from the Roman Reed Foundation, which promotes spinal cord injury research. "Dear @ladygaga how about using your celebrity status 2 try 2 get us out of wheelchairs. Instead of cruising one. Cool?!"[30]

"Was I offended she'd chosen to use a chair? No. I was momentarily jealous that hers was shinier than mine, and then I forgot about it," quipped Australian writer Stella Young. "I can't see that performing from a wheelchair while dressed as a mermaid makes any more comment on disability than arriving at the Grammys in an egg makes on chickens." Young pointed out that "some of the criticism that's been levelled at Gaga for her previous incorporations of mobility aids into her performance are based on the fact that there are a lot of very talented wheelchair dancers out there." She wonders if in future Gaga will incorporate some of them into her act. "Anything's possible with Gaga." She noted that "Opportunities for disabled actors to play high profile roles are so scarce, that it smarts a bit when we see non-disabled people in charge of them." Her tone was definitely inclusive when she added: "Gaga, you can borrow my beloved chair for your next show, if I can borrow your egg for my next red carpet arrival. Deal?"[31]

MORE SOCIAL MEDIA TO CONQUER

What made Lady Gaga one of the most influential celebrities in the world for 2011? It wasn't just income. Several of the top celebrities made far more income from their performances and recordings than Gaga did in 2011. It was her presence on social media websites such as YouTube, MySpace, Facebook, and especially Twitter that earned Gaga so much recognition from her fans and from the public at large.

"After having conquered Twitter, Facebook and YouTube, Lady Gaga appears to have her eye on adding the blogging platform Tumblr to her social media empire," commented Matthew Perpetua for *Rolling Stone*'s online magazine.[32] *Amen Fashion*, the name of her new blog, is based on a song lyric from her second album, *Born This Way*. For the first couple of months, most of the posts on *Amen Fashion* are photos of Gaga arriving or leaving somewhere unspecified, with a brief caption specifying the designer of her gloves, gown, or shoes. Photos aren't ideally suited to Twitter posting, but are an excellent element for a chatty, slice-of-real-life blog.

Other forms of electronic self-promotion and self-publishing are as useful as social media and come with greater bandwidth. Though Gaga does not yet have a Sirius satellite radio show of her own, Lüc Carl is branching out into that media. "Gaga stressed that Carl is still her best friend, sidestepping the boyfriend issue once again," noted

Lady Gaga performs on ABC's Good Morning America *in Central Park on May 27, 2011, in New York. (AP Photo/Evan Agostini)*

Gil Kaufman for MTV, "and that he's going to launch a Sirius satellite radio show soon."[33]

"I have this weird sick sense, not sixth sense but sick," she told *eTalk*'s host Ben Mulroney when he saw her just before going onstage in Toronto in 2011. "Like my fans are a disease that I don't ever want to recover from."

NOTES

1. Kaufman, Gil. "Lady Gaga Dishes on Sex, Drugs, Born This Way on Stern." *MTV.* Posted July 18, 2011. Retrieved July 20, 2011. http://www.mtv.com/news/articles/1667402/lady-gaga-howard-stern-born-this-way.jhtml.

2. Callahan, Maureen. "I Am Living for You Right Now." *Poker Face: The Rise and Rise of Lady Gaga.* New York: Hyperion/HarperCollins, 2010, p. 135.

3. Ibid.

4. Kreps, Daniel. "Lady Gaga Names Her New Album 'Born This Way.'" *Rolling Stone*. Posted September 13, 2010. Retrieved April 15, 2011. http://www.rollingstone.com/music/news/lady-gaga-names-her-new-album-born-this-way-20100913.

5. Cooke, C. W., Dan Glasl, and Adam Ellis. *Fame: Lady Gaga Vol. 2*. Vancouver, WA: Bluewater Productions, 2011, promotional statement.

6. Rafter, Dan, and Tess Fowler. *Fame: Lady Gaga*. Vancouver, WA: Bluewater Productions, 2010, promotional statement.

7. "Lady Gaga & Armani Strike Multimillion Dollar Deal." *The Huffington Post*. Posted September 27, 2010. Retrieved March 4, 2011. http://www.huffingtonpost.com/2010/09/27/lady-gaga-armani-deal_n_740774.html.

8. Armstrong, Denis. "Concert Review: Lady Gaga Scotiabank Place, Ottawa—March 7, 2011." *Jam*. Posted March 8, 2011. Retrieved March 13, 2011. http://jam.canoe.ca/Music/Artists/L/Lady_GaGa/ConcertReviews/2011/03/08/17532381.html.

9. Saxberg, Lynn. "Review, Gallery: Lady Gaga Lets Loose in Ottawa." *The Ottawa Citizen*. Posted March 7, 2011. Retrieved March 13, 2011. http://www.ottawacitizen.com/entertainment/Concert+review+Lady+Gaga+lets+loose+Ottawa/4395609/story.html. Page no longer available.

10. Ibid.

11. Kaufman, Gil. "Lady Gaga Lands in 'Guinness World Records' Book." *MTV.com*. Posted September 16, 2010. Retrieved May 3, 2011. http://www.mtv.com/news/articles/1647973/lady-gaga-lands-guinness-world-records-book.jhtml.

12. Thomson, Graeme. "Lady Gaga: The Future of Pop." *The Observer*. Posted November 29, 2009. Retrieved April 20, 2011. http://www.guardian.co.uk/music/2009/nov/29/lady-gaga-interview.

13. Martin, Dan. "The Lady Gaga Backlash Begins." *The Guardian Music Blog*. Posted April 20, 2011. Retrieved April 20, 2011. http://www.guardian.co.uk/music/musicblog/2011/apr/20/lady-gaga-backlash-begins?intcmp=239.

14. Kaufman, "Lady Gaga Dishes on Sex, Drugs, Born This Way on Stern."

15. Everett-Green, Rupert. "Lurid, Bitter, Swaggering, Maternal—and Oddly Real." Globe Arts. *The Globe and Mail*. March 5, 2011, p. R2.

16. Odell, Amy. "Lady Gaga on Texting Anna Wintour, Anderson Cooper on Child Modeling, and More Highlights from the CFDA Awards." *New York Fashion*. Posted June 7, 2011. Retrieved June 7, 2011. http://nymag.com/daily/fashion/2011/06/lady_gaga_on_texting_anna_wint.html.

17. Lady Gaga. *Facebook*. Posted June 7, 2011. Retrieved June 7, 2011. http://www.facebook.com/ladygaga.

18. Lady Gaga. *Twitter*. Posted May 16, 2011. Retrieved May 24, 2011. http://twitter.com/#!/ladygaga.

19. Lady Gaga. *Twitter*. Posted March 9, 2011. Retrieved April 10, 2011. http://twitter.com/ladygaga.

20. Lady Gaga. *Twitter*. Posted May 3, 2011. Retrieved May 24, 2011. http://twitter.com/#!/ladygaga.

21. Pomerantz, Dorothy. "Lady Gaga Tops Celebrity 100 List." *Forbes*. Posted May 18, 2011. Retrieved May 18, 2011. http://www.forbes.com/2011/05/16/lady-gaga-tops-celebrity-100–11.html. Page no longer available.

22. Lady Gaga. *Facebook*. Posted June 7, 2011. Retrieved June 7, 2011. http://www.facebook.com/ladygaga.

23. Ibid.

24. Lady Gaga. *Twitter*. Posted May 17, 2011. Retrieved May 24, 2011. http://twitter.com/#!/ladygaga.

25. Lady Gaga. "David Letterman Interview." *LadyGaga.com*. Posted May 24, 2011. Retrieved May 25, 2011. http://www.ladygaga.com/news/default.aspx?nid=35567. Page no longer available.

26. Chukerman, Brett. "Lady Gaga's Mermaid Troubles Continue." *Yahoo! Contributor Network*. Posted July 19, 2011. Retrieved July 20, 2011. http://omg.yahoo.com/news/lady-gagas-mermaid-troubles-continue/67530. Page no longer available.

27. Michaels, Sean. "Bette Midler Accuses Lady Gaga of Copying Her Act." *The Guardian*. Posted July 20, 2011. Retrieved July 21, 2011. http://www.guardian.co.uk/music/2011/jul/20/bette-midler-lady-gaga?intcmp=239.

28. Chukerman, "Lady Gaga's Mermaid Troubles Continue."

29. Michaels, "Bette Midler Accuses Lady Gaga of Copying Her Act."

30. @spinalcordcure. *Twitter*. Posted July 19, 2011. Retrieved August 25, 2011. http://twitter.com/#%21/spinalcordcure/status/91298429610889216.

31. Young, Stella. "Going Gaga Over Wheels." *Ramp Up*. Posted July 15, 2011. Retrieved July 20, 20 11. http://www.abc.net.au/rampup/articles/2011/07/15/3270307.htm.

32. Perpetua, Matthew. "Lady Gaga Launches 'Amen Fashion' Tumblr." *Rolling Stone*. Posted June 28, 2011. Retrieved July 28, 2011. http://www.rollingstone.com/music/news/lady-gaga-launches-amen-fashion-tumblr-20110628.

33. Kaufman, "Lady Gaga Dishes on Sex, Drugs, Born This Way on Stern."

Chapter 8

CHANGING THE WORLD, ONE SEQUIN AT A TIME

For a singer and songwriter, Lady Gaga seems to do a lot of just plain talking as well as performing. During her concerts, she addresses the audience between songs. During interviews, she speaks to reporters, interviewers, and fans with prepared answers to their questions. Sometimes an unguarded response comes to an unexpected question. But most of the time, Gaga seems to know exactly what she was planning to say. Recorded interviews almost always go exactly as they are planned by Gaga and her entourage.

Her agenda isn't only to be famous. What good does it hold being famous without being admired by people you respect? The rants and exhortations that Gaga makes during her concerts are calls to empower her fans to discover and celebrate themselves as she does.

Another of Gaga's goals is her charitable work. And as well as the comments that Lady Gaga makes about personal empowerment and helping others, she also makes statements of political commentary. The upshot of all these manifestos is the statement she made on her own website, and in many interviews: "I'm just trying to change the world one sequin at a time."

VIVA GLAM

The MAC Viva Glam campaign chooses a celebrity spokesperson at intervals, to be the face for their fund-raising programs for charity. One of the most controversial choices was the cross-dressing performer Ru-Paul. It was no surprise when Gaga was approached by MAC to be their new spokesperson for the campaign.

Gaga made appearances with Cyndi Lauper, promoting the new lipstick color as a fund-raiser for HIV and AIDS awareness programs. It meant a lot to Gaga that the color chosen was based on the Pink Nouveau shade that she'd worn for years as her default go-to lipstick for ordinary days. Both singers were impressed by the idea that the funded programs would put female condoms in the hands of women who couldn't otherwise afford them. Other celebrities supported the program as well.

"People take me both ways, way too seriously and not seriously enough," Gaga told Anderson Cooper and the 60 *Minutes* team. It did seem a little odd to see Gaga in public with minimal flamboyance, giving a serious and calm message about health. "I just want to use my position as a public figure to make people aware of what has happened," Gaga said. "I want to protect the precious and the perfect thing that is the little monsters." Later in that same prime-time special, she was shown making a statement at a 2009 awards ceremony. "I am wearing a latex pantsuit that is inspired by condoms because we are going to talk about safe sex," she said. "AIDS is 100% preventable but 0% curable." She spoke of the increasing rate at which people were being infected with the virus that leads to AIDS. An increasing number of women in particular were being infected with HIV. At least some of those infections could be blamed on ignorance and not taking time to think ahead. Perhaps the time it took to put on lipstick could be a moment for reflection and awareness, Gaga suggested in several brief video interviews, before intimacy could lead to infection.

GET OUT OF HELL FREE

There have been some demonstrations at concerts, where protestors carry signs condemning Lady Gaga. In her *Gagavision* video number 41, Gaga is shown talking through her car window with a protestor. He carried a sign saying "Trust in Christ or end in Hell!" "It's gonna happen one day, darlin'," he said. "I'm talking to you over here."

"I'm listening," she answered. "You know, we really believe in God at my show."

"Well, your pervert ways don't give any point to what God is all about," he said. "You know, the homo stuff." When she pointed out that she went to Catholic school for 13 years, he shook his head. "That's probably most of your problem. You got raised in a screwy religion."

Later, Gaga filmed herself at her mirrored dressing room table. "I think what's mostly confusing, is why he printed up these things," she said, holding up one of the protestor's Get Out of Hell Free cards that he had been distributing. "If it was so easy to get out of hell, why don't we just print up a bunch of these guys? It just makes me sad that my fans have to see that. But I know that's just part of what I'm supposed to do." The video then displays the words: "If you have revolutionary potential, then you have a moral imperative to make the world a better place."[1]

SELF-APPOINTED LIBERATOR

The craft website Etsy partnered with Lady Gaga and Sony/ATV Music Publishing to raise money and awareness for VH1 Save the Music Foundation by selling limited edition posters. "Lady Gaga has teamed with Etsy to raise money for VH1 Save the Music," crowed the singer's Facebook page in the summer of 2011. Her Facebook friends were exhorted to check out the Etsy store "to see the limited edition Born This Way-inspired designs by Etsy members, all signed by Gaga!"[2]

Other charity programs have Gaga's support as well. "BORN THIS WAY The Country Road Version is on iTunes now all purchases go to anti bullying charity www.glsen.org,"[3] Gaga tweeted a week after the release of the country version of her song. A country-style version of any Lady Gaga work might seem completely odd, but the roots of pop music are deep in folk music rather than in the modern forms of jazz and heavy metal rock. No matter how much Gaga herself likes listening to hair metal and grind rock, her own songwriting is pop and is structured so that a country sound doesn't contradict her original message.

"After researching Gaga's oeuvre, I realized two things," said writer and director Alistair Newton. "She is an appropriation artist in the tradition of Jasper Johns, firmly rooted in postmodern theorem. And she has positioned herself as a kind of Messianic liberator to her fans."[4]

"The nature of what I create is very polarizing. Public perception of me is the least important thing on my list," said Gaga, quoted on a fan's website. "Rumors, shots at me as a human being, that's what comes with the territory of being a musician and being someone who is a public figure. I care only about what I can change. What can I push forward? How can I be a part of the fight for modern social issues? How can I change young people's lives? How can I create a show and an album that is a portal to surreality, to free ourselves of all of our insecurities and to be proud of who we are? I'm a f**king hippie in that way, and that's just who I am."[5]

A REAL FEMINIST?

In several of her songs, Gaga writes of women who are "unreliable narrators, misunderstood or even unable to speak," observed journalist Ann Powers. In 2009, Gaga told a Norwegian journalist that she wasn't a feminist, adding that she loved men and hailed them. To a journalist from the *Los Angeles Times* a few months later, she said that she was "a little bit of a feminist."[6] Then she announced in *Rolling Stone* that she was a feminist, in response to a question from Neil Strauss about talking in a really brazenly sexual manner or dressing in ways that show a lot of skin.

Is Gaga a real feminist? The editors of the *Encyclopedia Britannica* consulted a philosophy professor for her opinion. "It's hard to know what to do with this question—or with the question of whether she's just pretending to be a feminist in order to make money," said Nancy Bauer. The mother of four teenaged children, Bauer was impressed by her 18-year-old daughter's analysis of the "Telephone" video. Her teenage daughter brought up questions that were similar to questions raised by Simone de Beauvoir in *The Second Sex*, dilemmas about how women manage contradictions and compromises in their lives. "The tensions and contradictions Gaga embodies are a hallmark of women's constrained situation."[7]

If Gaga really believes she is a feminist and that her displays show a kind of power, Bauer says that the pop star is "playing a tricky game: regardless of what she intends, her way of being in the world may come off as a glorification of simple self-objectification. It might send the message to other young women that it's a good idea for them to seek power, and self-empowerment, through deploying their sexuality strategically." Bauer admits that in fact, it still may be true that for women who want to make their way in the world, the surest bet is to exploit themselves sexually. "To me, feminism is about trying to move from such a world to a better one, in which women have more options," said Bauer. "The jury is still out, I think, on whether Lady Gaga's playing with her sexuality might count as a move in that direction."[8]

For years, Bauer has been thinking about how feminist philosophy can make itself pertinent in the real world. She believes that feminist philosophers ought to try to interest people in the project of continually reflecting on our settled opinions to improve our ability to make wise decisions, and genuinely care for ourselves and others. The challenge, as far as Bauer can tell, is to figure out the best, most honest way to try to attract people to that project. Gaga certainly does challenge settled opinions.

"Though she talks nonstop about liberation, Gaga's work abounds with images of violation and entrapment," wrote Ann Powers for the *Los Angeles Times*. She observed that in the 1980s, Madonna employed bondage imagery, and it felt sexual. But to Powers, when Gaga employs bondage imagery, it looks like it hurts. "She says she wants her fans to feel safe in expressing their imperfections. 'I want women—and men—to feel empowered by a deeper and more psychotic part of themselves. The part they're always trying desperately to hide. I want that to become something that they cherish.' But what is this freakishness, which she hopes to nurture?"[9]

TSUNAMI RELIEF

Shortly after the 2011 earthquake and tsunami in Japan, Gaga wrote notes of support on Twitter and Facebook. Her website soon had a note displayed about a fund-raising project for charity. "Lady Gaga designed a 'We Pray for Japan' prayer bracelet," said the website note. "Buy yours now for $5 in the web store and all proceeds go to Japan tsunami re-lief. You can also choose to add an additional donation with your pur-chase." On March 11, 2011, Lady Gaga's Facebook page had a new status posted: "I designed a Japan Prayer Bracelet. Buy It/Donate here and ALL proceeds will go to Tsunami Relief Efforts. Go Monsters" with the URL for the website. By March 14, the page was updated to read: "Monsters: in just 48 hrs you've raised a quarter of a million dollars for Japan Relief . . . It's important we help."

A lawsuit was filed in June, claiming that inflated shipping costs and sales tax were charged to the purchasers. The same day that the lawsuit was filed, Gaga was participating in a benefit concert for the Japanese Red Cross in Chiba City, Japan, organized by MTV Music Video Aid Japan. By that date, she claimed to have already donated about $3 mil-lion to Japanese relief programs.

A statement released by Gaga insisted that the lawsuit was with-out merit. "The entire $5 donation made with the purchase of each bracelet is going to support the disaster relief,"[11] said the statement. No profit was made on shipping costs, the statement went on to say, and any charges made for sales taxes were in accordance with local laws. By August, the bracelet was no longer available.

SCREAM FOR ICE CREAM

The most iconic image of nurturing is the idea of a mother nursing her child. But associating mother's milk with the Gaga phenomenon didn't work out so well for a London restaurant, The Icecreamists. In-form Music Network reported in March 2011 that lawyers representing Lady Gaga threatened legal proceedings against the restaurant. The offence? Making ice cream using breast milk. The milk was expressed by 15 women who replied to an advertisement posted by the restaurant on an online mothers' forum. The name chosen to market this new ice cream flavor was "Baby Gaga." Within days of going on sale, the first batch was a big hit in the trendy Covent Garden district and had sold out completely.

The pop icon's managers and representatives would not accept this encroachment on the trademarked Lady Gaga image. It's not certain whether the matter was ever brought to the attention of the singer herself. The law firm Mishcon de Reya sent a sternly worded letter to The Icecreamists Limited, advising the restaurant's owners to change the name of the ice cream if they wanted to avoid proceedings for trademark infringement.

"The letter accuses The Icecreamists of 'taking unfair advantage of, and riding on the coattails of' Lady Gaga's trademarks in a manner that is 'deliberately provocative and, to many people, nausea-inducing,'" noted a writer for the Inform Music Network. "Each serving costs 14 (pounds) and is brought out by waitresses wearing flamboyant costumes, something Lady Gaga is well-known for. But it is now off the menu after Westminster City Council, the local authority, seized the ice cream for health and safety checks."[12]

MEAT DRESS

Gaga's meat dress wasn't the first of its kind. Back in 1999, writer Ashley Seashore went to an exhibit at the Israel Art Museum that displayed a meat dress by Canadian artist Jana Sterbak. "It wasn't just the spectacle of a dress made of meat, it was the context," wrote Seashore. The dress wasn't displayed all by itself. It was one of several pieces in an exhibit that included the artists' commentary on superficiality and vanity, contrasting those attitudes with shelter, comfort, and security. "It made me think about the clothes I put on my body, and the nourishment I put into it," said Seashore. She quoted the artist Sterbak's statement: "The work also addresses issues concerning women, fashion, consumption, and the body. The equation of women with meat and the notion that 'you are what you wear' are common ideas in Western society."[13]

The day after parading in her meat dress at the 2010 MTV Video Music Awards, Gaga gave an explanation for the outfit to talk show host Ellen DeGeneres, who is a vegan. "It's certainly no disrespect to anyone that's vegan or vegetarian. As you know, I'm the most judgment-free human being on Earth," said Gaga. "It has many interpretations, but for me this evening it's [saying] if we don't stand up for what we believe in, if we don't fight for our rights, pretty soon we're going to have as much rights as the meat on our bones. And I am not meat."[14]

In Seashore's opinion, the loss of meaning of the original work is the real problem. "If you Google 'meat dress,' Lady Gaga occupies most of the search results, along with her banal, generic and self-serving . . . explanation about standing up for what we believe in," wrote Seashore. "The connection she makes between the meat dress and 'standing up for what we believe' is weak at best. I mean, *aren't* we the meat on our bones? Isn't that, like, our flesh?"

"Perhaps this crystallizes the growing argument that people have about Lady Gaga: that she's just a spectacle. I'm still on the fence about that," says Seashore. "I think she does tremendous and necessary work for the gay community. But in terms of what she does as an 'artist' . . . well, it seems that this particularly unoriginal statement only shows that the lady is swimming in the shallow end of the pool."[15]

The idea of wearing a meat dress seems to have become a synonym for Lady Gaga for some commentators. After the award ceremony, the meat of the costume wasn't simply discarded, nor was it barbecued. In an interview on *Late Night with David Letterman*, Gaga confirmed a rumor that the meat dress was turned into beef jerky to be preserved as an art object. The jerky was made by a friend. Gaga has many crafting skills, but so far making homemade beef jerky isn't one of them.

TELLING LEGISLATORS TO REPEAL DON'T ASK, DON'T TELL

"Equality is the prime rib of America," said Gaga at a televised protest rally in Portland, Maine, on September 20, 2010. "But because I'm gay I don't get to share the greatest cut of beef my country has to offer. There are amazing heroes here today, whose stories are more powerful than any I could tell, any fight I've ever fought, any song that I could sell. I'm here because they inspire me . . . I'm here because Don't Ask, Don't Tell is wrong. It's unjust. And fundamentally, it is against all that we stand for as Americans."

Even as fashion magazines and websites debate Lady Gaga's style and fashion sense, there's a lot of approval for her commentary on gender rights. "[T]here's no denying that she has done a fantastic job speaking out for LGBT rights. As someone who is so passionate about a positive approach to sexuality, she also made appearances with fellow LGBT activist Cyndi Lauper to talk about the importance of safe sex," wrote Lilit Marcus for fashion website *The Gloss*. "That's why we're incredibly disappointed to learn that Lady Gaga worked with photographer Terry Richardson, whom we exposed as a creep who intimidates and sexually harasses the models he works with."

Gaga's video message to the U.S. Senate regarding the Don't Ask, Don't Tell policy was shot by photographer Terry Richardson. He was also the photographer who took the images of Gaga in a meat dress for the cover of *Vogue Hommes Japan*.

"While it's great that Gaga has used her fame to take a stand on this issue, it's a shame that the person she chose to record her important message is someone who clearly doesn't value sexuality,"[16] wrote Marcus. She described the article posted on *The Gloss*, about a model's bad experience working for Richardson, which became a hot discussion topic in the media as other models came forward, and is even referenced on Richardson's Wikipedia page. Marcus feels that it's not difficult to find out Richardson's reputation. "[I]t's unfortunate that someone as feminist and pro-positive sexuality as Lady Gaga would choose to work with someone who doesn't seem to feel the same way when the sexuality in question is those of young women who model for him."

Marcus supports the work that Gaga is doing to promote a positive view toward sexuality and to repeal the Don't Ask, Don't Tell legislation, but she advises that Gaga should never work with Richardson in the future. It's hard to make an important public statement about sexual discrimination when that statement is shot by someone with a reputation for sexually harassing women. "The fashion industry continuing to give Richardson work is only sending the message that what he did was okay. Lady Gaga, you have the ability to change that message as well. You have the ability to tell young women that it's not acceptable for men in positions of authority to coerce them into sexual acts, and you can do that by denouncing Richardson and making sure you never work with him again. We're counting on you."

OFF TARGET

"Lady Gaga has ended her deal to sell an exclusive version of her new album, *Born This Way*, at Target," reported the *New York Post*. "The flamboyant singer is upset over the big-box retailer Target over its controversial political donations." It was the national gay and lesbian magazine *The Advocate* that originally made the public aware that Target had donated funds to several anti-gay politicians and organizations. Almost immediately, the big box store Target came under fire from citizen activist groups, and Gaga withdrew from the deal.

As Gaga explained to *Billboard.com* magazine last month, she had agreed to work with Target but now had to end the contract. "Part of my deal with Target is that they have to start affiliating themselves with LGBT charity groups and begin to reform and make amends for the mistakes they've made in the past," said Gaga in a quote from the *Post*. One of her representatives made the official statement that "Lady Gaga and Target came to a mutual decision to end their overall exclusive partnership."[17] Target made no response to the *Post*'s article.

HOT AIR

It seems wasteful and excessive for pop stars to use a lot of resources when they perform at large venues and tour the world in jet planes. Some of the performances are more environmentally conscious than others. The costumes that Gaga wears when performing, for example, may be excessive. But most of the costumes are not merely worn for a single performance, like the meat dress. Dresses and accessories that appear in her videos are reused onstage when performing, particularly garments handmade by the *Haus of Gaga*. The basic three R's of environmentalism are reduce, reuse, and recycle.

There may be a lot of garments in Lady Gaga's wardrobe, but she gets a lot of use out of most of her wardrobe. It doesn't take much work to track a single garment, such as the miniskirted nun's habit in see-through plastic, from one appearance to another in paparazzi photographs outside meetings in restaurants, through dance videos and onstage performances in arenas and music festivals.

Music festivals aren't just a picnic in the park, where a few dozen people sit on blankets listening to a singer with an acoustic guitar. There are stages and speakers, refreshments and toilet facilities. Oxford University released research that showed that the greenhouse gas emissions "from 500 festivals in the UK was 84,000 tonnes [about 85,000 metric tons] of carbon dioxide in one year."[18] That's more than the annual carbon footprint of several small countries. And it's all for music.

In Great Britain, 10 music festivals joined a campaign to cut their greenhouse gas emissions by 10 percent during 2010. The 10:10 campaign in the United Kingdom was part of a series of similar efforts internationally. At these music festivals, Lady Gaga was one of the performers.

"All you need is love and art and each other,"[19] Gaga told the crowd when performing an acoustic version of "Poker Face" at Oxegen Festival in Dublin. Eamon Ryan, the Irish minister for communications, energy and natural resources, praised the festival for its efforts to be "sustainable, green and fun."[20] Oxegen 2009 was considered to be the largest 100 percent carbon-neutral event to take place that year in Ireland.

In 2011, there were protests all summer at music events. "Musicians including Lady Gaga, Korn, Disturbed, Godsmack, Creed, and the Backstreet Boys said they planned to boycott BP [British Petroleum] on their national tours this year," said an article in London's *Guardian* newspaper. "The oil industry has been a target for artists and activists for many years." The scientists campaigning for public awareness of climate change now have Gaga and other performers on their team. "Climate change activists, artists and musicians opposed to the fossil fuel industry are determined to highlight BP's link to the arts in the context of the company's international embarrassment over the continuing oil spill in the gulf of Mexico," wrote journalists John Vidal and Owen Bowcott. "The calls for cultural institutions to distance themselves from the oil industry come at a time when government spending on the arts is about to be slashed amid efforts to cut public debt."[21]

MISSING A BEAT

Moments of political commentary have begun to appear in Gaga's stage shows. Sometimes her words bring a warm response from the audience. Sometimes her political gestures are an error rather than a rallying point for the crowd.

One of the political outrages occurred at the opening of her concert in Belfast, Northern Ireland, on October 30, 2010. Using the green, white, and orange flag of the Republic of Ireland as a prop was not a smooth move, especially not when she raised the middle finger on her other hand. "I just felt it was inappropriate," said a fan, "but maybe she didn't realize Northern Ireland is separate from the Republic."[22]

Though she said nothing about the flag during her show, Gaga leaned back in her black bikini costume and used the flag and its pole as a sexual prop. Reactions were mixed among the crowd of 10,000 people. "Silly Gaga, check your geography before whipping out flags!"[23] quipped a commentator for *Irish Central* online magazine. "Loyalist fans branded her decision 'inappropriate' and 'disgusting,'"[24] reported Jessica Brown for a U.K. newspaper.

There was far less controversy over Gaga biting the head off a Barbie doll during the same show, then rubbing the doll over the studded crotch on her black leather bikini. That act was a moment that paid tribute to rocker Ozzy Osborne. Knowing what sexual props will offend a particular audience means knowing the tastes and style appreciated by people in the location she is performing each day. It's not an easy thing to do, to keep track of opinions that change as Gaga moves around the world on tour.

NOT BORN THIS WAY IN MALAY

The popularity of Lady Gaga is not limited to Western nations. Her overseas tours with the Pussycat Dolls and New Kids on the Block, and later her own Fame Ball tour and Monster Ball tour have earned her millions of dedicated fans who have seen her perform in person. As well, broadcasts on radio and television keep her reputation alive in cities and towns around the world. One of the private television stations in Malaysia, 8TV, targets younger viewers by presenting Chinese programming in the first session of each broadcast, and English language programming in the second session of each broadcast.

Almost as soon as Gaga's song "Born This Way" was released, it could be tracked heading for the top of the charts internationally. The song was popular on radio stations around the world. In Malaysia, radio stations played "Born This Way" when it was released. But some of the lyrics were deliberately garbled during the broadcasts. Specifically, the garbled words were: "No matter gay, straight or bi, lesbian, transgendered life, I'm on the right track baby, I was born to survive."[25]

The top private operator in Malaysia, AMP Radio Networks, released a statement suggesting that the lyrics might be offensive. "The particular lyrics in 'Born This Way' may be considered offensive when viewed against Malaysia's social and religious observances," the company said. "The issue of being gay, lesbian or [bisexual] is still considered as a 'taboo' by general Malaysians."[26]

It may be hard for music fans in Western countries to understand the decision of radio stations to garble that line in a hit song. When a Canadian or American radio station censors words in a song, the words are usually violent or sexually explicit. But in Malaysia, there are government censorship rules against the promotion of being gay.

"Homosexuality is not specified as a crime in Malaysia, but there is a law prohibiting sodomy, which is punishable by up to 20 years in prison and whipping,"[27] reported an Associated Press article in the British newspaper *The Guardian*. Alternative sexual orientations are not allowed to be presented in Malaysian media. Broadcasters are subject to fines and other penalties if they present song lyrics like those in "Born This Way."

On March 22, 2011, Gaga was interviewed about her opinion of the censorship of Malaysian broadcasts of her song. "Well, obviously I disagree with it, otherwise I wouldn't have specifically put those words in a song I knew would be put on top forty radio," said Gaga in response to a fan's question. "For all the young people in Malaysia that want those words to be played on the radio, it is your job and it is your duty as young people to have your voices heard."[28]

That's not a bad directive for Gaga to give her North American or European fans. But in other countries, speaking out against artistic censorship laws can have severe consequences. When police in other countries arrest people under censorship laws, the accused people can end up with criminal records, beaten, or jailed.

As time goes by, Gaga's appeal to young people in Malaysia may have different results for her fans in that largely Muslim country than it would for fans in a Western nation. It's not unusual for arrests to occur in Malaysia after a show. A Muslim singer and her band were arrested in 2007 after performing in a Malaysian nightclub. The singer, Siti Noor Idayu Abd Moin, was fined and held overnight on charges of "revealing her body" and "promoting vice"[29] for wearing long trousers and a sleeveless top that showed part of her back.

"Malaysia's authorities are no strangers to protecting public morals against pop stars," wrote journalist Ian MacKinnon. He noted that in 2006, "organizers of a concert by the US act Pussycat Dolls were fined for allowing the all-girl band to perform a sexually suggestive routine while wearing revealing outfits."[30] During that tour, Gaga was one of the performers. It's no news to Gaga that racy song lyrics or provocative stage performances are illegal in Malaysia. The lyrics of "Born This Way" were written deliberately, to provoke a response from countries with censorship laws.

In spite of these arrests in Malaysia, Gaga does not advise that her Malaysian fans stay silent in the face of censorship. "You must do everything that you can if you want to be liberated by your society. You must call, you must not stop, you must protest peaceably, no violence," she insisted. "I don't believe in negativity. There's no reason to be derogatory. You just have to keep fighting for what you believe in."[31]

It was a strangely passionate call to duty. Did she want them to save the world or hear a pop song? Gaga made this appeal at a time when public demonstrations were having unusually strong effects in Muslim countries around the world. The president of Tunisia resigned in January 2011 after "a month of violent demonstrations over worsening economic corruption, and political repression."[32] During that month, a Tunisian rap singer was arrested and jailed for two days for a song he released online. "The song 'President, your people are dying' is about problems facing youth and unemployment," wrote journalist George Stromboupolous.[33]

The results of peaceable protests cannot always be predicted. Eighteen days of public protests forced the Egyptian dictator Hosni Mubarak to resign on February 11, 2011.[34] A few weeks later, similar demonstrations in Libya against the dictator Muammar Gaddafi were met by anti-aircraft guns fired by the military; on March 18, the United Nations declared a no-fly zone over the parts of Libya affected by the violence.[35] Just three days before Gaga called for nonviolent demonstrations in Malaysia, over 50 protesters in Yemen were killed by government snipers after their midday prayers.[36] That same week, other protesters in Syria and Bahrain were being killed by government forces.[37]

The long summer of 2011 showed that political unrest in Muslim countries was not well served by artistic calls to action. But silence from public figures is not a responsible action either. The actions and phrasing that succeed in Western nations do not always have the same desired effects in other countries. It is at moments like this that Lady Gaga's relative youth and inexperience become more apparent.

BRINGING THE FUTURE

The Lady Gaga stage persona is that of a confident and powerful woman who succeeds when struggling against fantasy situations. She projects this same persona offstage as well. But Gaga's appeal to her fans in Malaysia to liberate themselves peacefully shows that in many ways, she is still a very young and inexperienced person. By the age of 26, she has traveled the world, to every continent except Antarctica. She has performed before royalty and the president of the United States. She has phenomenal success in her business. But she hasn't completed a diploma or a bachelor's degree. She hasn't married or had children yet. As for ordinary working life, Gaga couldn't even keep a job as a waitress for more than a few weeks, when she was a high-school sophomore. All her experience since age 13 or 14 has been focused on performing and songwriting. It's hard work, but there's little in common with an ordinary job.

Gaga is already behaving as if she were an empowering figurehead for millions of people. It will take more hands-on experience in the world of ordinary life as well as the performing arts for Gaga to become truly the empowering figurehead that she is already behaving like. Based on her track record of behaving as if she were an artistic superstar and then becoming one in truth, her future will be well worth watching.

NOTES

1. Lady Gaga. *Gagavision video number 41*. Retrieved June 24, 2011. http://www.youtube.com/user/ladygagaofficial?blend=2&ob=4#p/f/1/wrOYFZwmMUM.

2. Lady Gaga. *Facebook*. Posted June 7, 2011. Retrieved June 7, 2011. http://www.facebook.com/ladygaga.

3. Lady Gaga. *Twitter*. Posted April 5, 2011. Retrieved April 10, 2011. http://twitter.com/ladygaga.

4. Nestruck, J. Kelly. "Rhubarb Festival: Lady Gaga Gets a Musical of Sorts." Arts. *The Globe and Mail*. Posted February 16, 2011. Retrieved February 21, 2011. http://w ww.theglobeandmail.com/news/arts/theatre/nestruck-on-theatre/rhubarb-festival-lady-gaga-gets-a-musical-of-sorts/article1910318/.

5. Kinser, Jeremy. "Portrait of a Lady." *The Advocate*. Posted July 5, 2011. Retrieved November 13, 2011. http://news.advocate.com/post/7263991145/lady-gaga-portrait-of-a-lady.

6. Powers, Ann. "Frank talk with Lady Gaga." *Los Angeles Times*. Posted December 13, 2009. Retrieved April 9, 2011. http://www.latimes.com/entertainment/news/music/la-ca-lady-gaga13-2009dec13,0,632518,full.story.

7. Levy, Michael. "Is Lady Gaga a Feminist? 5 Questions for Philosopher Nancy Bauer." *Encyclopedia Britannica*. Posted July 26, 2010. Retrieved April 9, 2011. http://www.britannica.com/blogs/2010/07/is-lady-gaga-a-feminist-5-questions-for-philosopher-nancy-bauer/.

8. Ibid.

9. Powers, "Frank talk with Lady Gaga."

10. Trivett, Vincent. "Lady Gaga Sued Over Japan Relief Bracelets." *Business Insider*. Posted June 27, 2011. Retrieved June 30, 2011. http://articles.businessinsider.com/2011-06-27/entertainment/30070766_1_lady-gaga-benefit-concert-law-firm.

11. Serjeant, Jill. "Lady Gaga Vehemently Denies Japan Charity Bracelet Scam." *Bilboard.biz*. Posted June 29, 2011. Retrieved June 30, 2011. http://www.billboard.biz/bbbiz/industry/legal-and-management/lady-gaga-vehemently-denies-japan-charity-1005255952.story.

12. AFP. "Lady Gaga Eyes Legal Action over Breast Milk Ice Cream." *Inform Music Network*. Posted March 6, 2011. Retrieved March 13, 2011. http://informmusicnetwork.com/music-stars/lady-gaga-eyes-legal-action-breast-milk-ice-cream-4750389a.

13. Seashore, Ashley. "Lady Gaga's Meat Dress and the Question of Authenticity." *The Gloss*. Posted September 13, 2010. Retrieved March 16, 2011. http://thegloss.com/culture/lady-gagas-meat-dress-and-the-question-of-authenticity/.

14. "Lady Gaga Laughs off Meat Controversy." *Metrolyrics*. Posted September 19, 2010. Retrieved November 13, 2011. http://www.metrolyr ics.com/2010-lady-gaga-laughs-off-meat-dress-criticism-news.html.

15. Seashore, op.cit.

16. Marcus, Lilit. "Dear Lady Gaga, You Shouldn't Have Worked with Terry Richardson." *The Gloss*. Posted September 20, 2010. Retrieved March 16, 2011. http://thegloss.com/culture/dear-lady-gaga-you-shouldnt-have-worked-with-terry-richardson/.

17. NewsCore. "Lady Gaga Falls Out with Target over Anti-Gay Donations." *CourierMail*. Posted March 14, 2011. Retrieved March 13, 2011. http://www.couriermail.com.au/entertainment/confidential/lady-gaga-falls-out-with-target-over-anti-gay-donations/story-e6freq7o-1226020897015.

18. Jowitt, Juliette. "UK Music Festivals Join 10:10 Campaign to Cut Emissions." *The Guardian*. Posted June 7, 2010. Retrieved April 14, 2011. http://www.guardian.co.uk/environment/2010/jun/07/uk-music-festivals-10–10?INTCMP=SRCH. Page no longer available.

19. HausOfGagaDaily. "Lady Gaga—Poker Face (Acoustic Version Live at Oxegen Festival 2009." *YouTube*. Posted August 5, 2009. Retrieved June 5, 2011. http://www.youtube.com/watch?v=xjY0jphu BA0&NR=1.

20. "Fleetwood Mac to Play Dublin." *The Irish Times*. Posted June 4, 2009. Retrieved June 5, 2011. http://www.irishtimes.com/newspaper/breaking/2009/0604/breaking29.html.

21. Vidal, John, and Owen Bowcott. "Galleries and Museums Face Summer of Protest over BP Arts Sponsorship." *The Guardian*. Posted June 24, 2010. Retrieved April 14, 2011. http://www.guardian.co.uk/environment/2010/jun/24/galleries-museums-summer-protest-bp-arts-sponsorship?INTCMP=SRCH.

22. Andrews, Amy. "Lady Gaga Uses Tricolor for Belfast Gig to Dismay of Fans." *Irish Central*. Posted November 2, 2010. Retrieved April 5, 2010. http://www.irishcentral.com/story/ent/amyandrews_gossipgirl/lady-gaga-uses-tricolor-for-belfast-gig-to-dismay-of-fans-106516063.html.

23. Ibid.

24. Brown, Jessica, and Sonja Stephen. "Lady Gaga: I'm Going to Give Up the Ghost!" *Daily Star*. Posted November 3, 2010. Retrieved

April 5, 2011. http://www.dailystar.co.uk/playlist/view/161244/Lady-GaGa-I-m-going-to-give-up-the-ghost-/.

25. Garibay, Fernando, Paul Blair, Stefani Germanotta, and Jeppe Breum Laursen. "Born This Way." *Ladygaga.com*. Retrieved March 27, 2011. http://www.ladygaga.com/lyrics/default.aspx?tid=23051878.

26. On Top Magazine Staff. "Lady Gaga Urges Malaysians to Protest Censorship of Gay Anthem 'Born This Way.'" *On Top Magazine*. Posted March 24, 2011. Retrieved March 24, 2011. http://www.ontopmag.com/article.aspx?id=7903&MediaType=1&Category=22.

27. AP. "Malaysian Police Arrest 37 at Gay Sex Party." *The Guardian*. Posted November 6, 2007. Retrieved March 25, 2011. http://www.guardian.co.uk/world/2007/nov/06/gayrights.malaysia?INTCMP=ILCNETTXT3487.

28. On Top Magazine Staff, "Lady Gaga Urges Malaysians to Protest Censorship of Gay Anthem 'Born This Way.'"

29. MacKinnon, Ian. "Malaysian Singer Arrested for Wearing 'Revealing Top.'" *The Guardian*. Posted July 6, 2007. Retrieved March 25, 2011. http://www.guardian.co.uk/world/2007/jul/06/musicnews.malaysia.

30. Ibid.

31. On Top Magazine Staff, "Lady Gaga Urges Malaysians to Protest Censorship of Gay Anthem 'Born This Way.'"

32. CBC News. "MAP: Protests Spread in Middle East." *CBC News World*. Posted January 26, 2011. Retrieved March 24, 2011. http://www.cbc.ca/news/world/story/2011/01/26/f-unrest-north-africa-middle-east.html.

33. Stromboupolous, George. "Update: Tunisian Rapper Arrested for Protest Song Now Released." *CBC.ca*. Posted January 7, 2011, updated January 9, 2011. Retrieved March 24, 2011. http://www.cbc.ca/strombo/george-feed/music-1/tunisian-rapper-arrested-for-protest-song.html.

34. CBC News. "Egyptian Protesters Rejoice at Mubarak's Ouster." *CBC News World*. Posted February 11, 2011. Retrieved March 24, 2011. http://www.cbc.ca/news/world/story/2011/02/11/egypt-mubarak-future.html.

35. CBC news. "Harper Heads to Paris Meeting on Libya." *Sympatico.ca*. Posted March 18, 2011. Retrieved March 24, 2011. http://

news.sympatico.cbc.ca/home/canada_will_help_enforce_libya_no-fly_zone_pm/984eefed. Page no longer available.

36. Macdonald, Neil. "Libya, Yemen, Syria: The Hierarchy of Despotism." *CBC News World.* Posted March 23, 2011. Retrieved March 24, 2011. http://www.cbc.ca/news/world/story/2011/03/23/f-rfa-macdonald.html.

37. Hughes, Michael. "Mideast Protest Update: Yemen, Syria, Saudi Arabia, Bahrain." *Examiner.com.* Posted March 21, 2011. Retrieved March 24, 2011. http://www.examiner.com/geopolitics-in-national/mideast-protest-update-yemen-syria-saudi-arabia-bahrain?utm_source=twitterfeed&utm_medium=twitter.

Chapter 9

PLANS FOR THE FUTURE

The journey isn't over yet for Lady Gaga. Even at her young age, she's been asked in interviews to sum up her experiences so far. "It's been incredible. Truthfully, I'm just very grateful, and I can't work hard enough," Gaga told a British reporter. "I've been traveling so much, I've written songs in every continent around the world, and it's been so inspiring. I love it all, and it's only made me more hungry."[1]

A WORLDWIDE SENSATION

Before becoming a first-ranked pop star at home in America, Gaga was a sensation in many other countries. "Unless you've been living with the uncontacted tribes in Peru, you've probably noticed pop sensation Lady Gaga has become this generation's Madonna," commented Scott Tunstall for a media website. "Slightly attractive, moderately talented and vastly overexposed, Gaga is a hit machine and media magnet."[2]

When the album *Born This Way* was released in Brazil, in days it overtook the previous number one selling album. "It is outselling the rest of the Top 30 combined,"[3] wrote a Brazilian blogger.

The Lady Gaga phenomenon is truly worldwide. Even in Mongolia, it's possible to find fans of the performer and her music. When journalist Brian Awehali spent months in Mongolia in 2010, writing about multinational mining companies, he stayed for two weeks in the equivalent of a bed-and-breakfast outside the capital city Ulaanbataar. In a two hours' drive outside the city, Awehali was able to hire room and board in the *ger* (a felted wool tent also called a *yurt*) of a nomadic family.

"I . . . learned, through sharing my MP3 player with them, that Baul and his family really like the music of Lady Gaga," said Awehali. "Mines and markets may be swayed or stalled, but resistance to Gaga is futile. Pop culture is just one of the ways that Mongolia's nomadic herders are connected to the broader world."[4]

HEADLINING WITH OPRAH

"Lady Gaga is like the upcoming American woman but from, like, outer space," said model Coco Rocha at a 2010 gala at the Metropolitan Opera House in New York.

When Jonathan van Meter wrote about that gala, he called Gaga "a bizarre and brilliant and peculiarly American pastiche of seemingly every woman and a few men, most obviously Madonna, Cher, and Elton John." He spoke of "her strange accent, part Naomi Campbell-British, part nasal New York-Italian girl." Oprah came out when the show was delayed. "The reason we are delayed here is because Lady Gaga and her team are in the back praying before they perform," Oprah said to the waiting crowd at the gala. It wasn't just diva behavior. Gaga was frantically nervous about performing in front of Bono and Mick Jagger. "Because she understands that what they are doing is more than just art," said Oprah. "This is somebody who is saying to the world, 'Be the best that you are.' And so what she represents is the best in all of us, the identity of the American woman and our ability to be able to look inside of ourselves and *not* say 'I want to be like you, I want to be like you, I want to be like you,' but 'I want to be more of *myself*.' "[5]

It looks like Oprah is Gaga's biggest fan. Gaga appeared on the final Oprah "Harpo Hookups" show on May 5, 2011. Wearing a black coolie hat and red jacket with padded shoulders over a sheer black lace body stocking, Gaga hid her face with a mask made of blonde and black hair swirls. She sang a medley of her songs "Born This Way" and "Yoü and I" on a fantasy piano. Her voice had a new growl, a powerful howl absent from the album recordings of these songs.

To get down from the fantasy piano, Gaga needed a hand from her band members. The keyboard was elevated some eight feet above the stage in a sculpture wrapped with brassy wire till it looked like a great shoe. The sculpture was created by Natali Germanotta. Gaga's younger sister, at 19 years of age, is a fashion student who created the sculpture as a project. "To surprise her," Gaga told Oprah, "I had the sculpture made into a piano. So surprise, Natali!"[6]

RUNNING THE RED QUEEN'S RACE

"Her public persona is among the most heavily crafted in pop, yet on that stage, surrounded by her fans, you got the feeling that everything was for real," commented a Canadian writer, "including the haunted house inside the mind of Lady Gaga, who is a huge success in every worldly way, but is still spooked by the ghosts of old disappointments."[7]

Performing is her goal, not profiting from her hard work. "It means everything. It's all I want to do. I went completely bankrupt after the first leg of the Monster Ball tour," she admitted to *eTalk* host Ben Mulroney on a prime-time television special: *Lady Gaga—Born This Way.* "My manager told me, if you do this stage, if you do this tour, you will be three million dollars in debt. I said, just keep me on tour. I'll work it off." Her father called her, panicking, and she said, "Dad, just trust me." That explains the frenetic series of performances, as the Monster Ball tour seemed never-ending. "I really don't do this for the money."

Photographs of Gaga in *Vogue* in 2010 showed that the singer's hazel eyes had become sunken and hollow, compared with photos taken in 2008 and 2009. She also appears to be nesting, having invested in real estate in 2010. The eco-friendly, beach-front house she had built on the small island of Chappaquiddick has eight bedrooms, tennis courts, and a swimming pool. It'll take a lot of planning for her to make time in her busy schedule to relax there, a little ferry ride away from Martha's Vineyard.

"So invested is she in her onstage persona, for the sake of her fans, Lady Gaga says she won't even hydrate during a performance," reported journalist Simon Cable. He quoted her as saying: "I don't even drink water onstage in front of anybody, because I want them to focus on the fantasy of the music."[8]

"If I were to ever, God forbid, get hurt onstage and my fans were screaming outside of the hospital, waiting for me to come out, I'd come out as Gaga," she says, adding that she models her celebrity on Michael Jackson. "Michael got burned, and he lifted that glittered glove so damn high so his fans could see him, because he was in the art of show business. That's what we do."[9]

For the future? "If I had to give it all back, but got to keep my fans, that'd be ok,"[10] sighed Gaga on Twitter.

PARODY

Managers handle a lot of issues that never cross the mind of most artists. But sometimes the choices made by a manager aren't the choices that Gaga would prefer. One of the times her manager handled a decision without consulting her resulted in an abrupt reversal of his decision. At issue was a parody of her song "Born This Way."

You know you've really arrived as a pop singer, when "Weird Al" Yankovic records a parody of your hit song. "The cliché is that imitation is the highest form of flattery," commented journalist Joseph Alexiou. "If Weird Al, especially, wants to parody your song, then you've made it."[11] As a satirist, Al Yankovic writes songs with lyrics that comment on a variety of current events and cultural trends including films and news reports. His favorite targets are pop singers and rock stars. All the promotional hype surrounding performers makes them obvious examples for Yankovic's efforts to skewer popular culture.

"It's really an honor when he does that," said rapper Chamillionaire about the parody that Yankovic recorded of his own song "Ridin'," adding that "Weird Al is not gonna do a parody of your song if you're not doing it big. You gotta be a big dog."[12]

For his 2011 album, Yankovic was inspired to write a parody song that lampoons Gaga's song "Born This Way." Parodies of this sort are usually considered fair use or fair comment under copyright law in the

United States. Even so, before releasing an album with a recording of a parody song, Yankovic makes sure to contact the artists who composed and performed the original.

The usual response to his contact is good-natured acceptance of the joke. For instance, Michael Jackson enjoyed Yankovic's 1984 parody of "Beat It." He liked it so much that later, when Yankovic recorded a parody of "Bad" in 1988, Jackson loaned him a restored set to film a parody video.

But when Yankovic contacted Gaga's manager, the response was not so positive. Before okaying the release of a recording, Gaga would have to hear the parody first. Reading the lyrics was not enough. Yankovic hustled to get the recording done quickly, only to be told that Gaga didn't approve of the parody.

Disappointed, Yankovic wrote on his blog that because Gaga didn't approve, he would not release the parody on his next album. He did make the parody available for free on YouTube, and the positive response was immediate from fans and from Gaga herself.

"There must have been a misunderstanding because [Gaga] is in no way trying to block the release of the parody," sources close to Gaga insisted to online magazine *Three Mile Zone*. "She's busy touring and hasn't heard the song yet. Her manager hasn't had a chance to play it for her yet . . . She's a huge Weird Al fan."[13]

On his website, a delighted Yankovic updated his blog with the news that the parody would be available on his album and a video. "All my proceeds from the song and the video will go to the Human Rights Campaign,"[14] he promised, because of the original song's positive theme of diversity.

"One of the hardest things I've had to deal with in my career is keeping my material topical even though I only release albums every three or four years," Yankovic told *Billboard* magazine. "Now, with the advent and popularity of digital distribution, I don't have to wait around while my songs get old and dated—I can get them out on the Internet almost immediately."[15]

THE ECONOMICS OF SUPERSTARS

"There are millions of starving artists in the world, like the singer at your local pub who can barely make rent," observed journalist Tony Keller for

Report on Business. "Yet Lady Gaga made an estimated $62 million last year [2009]. How come?"

Keller solved the riddle of why some people are paid thousands of times an ordinary wage, which was explored by Sherwin Rosen, an economist at the University of Chicago. In Rosen's 1981 paper "The Economics of Superstars," Keller found an explanation for "why Lady Gaga doesn't have to be 5,000 times better than the local musician in order to earn 5,000 times more." There are two main factors. One is imperfect substitution: people are willing to pay a lot more for something only a little better than the usual. The other factor is joint consumption technologies that allow millions of people to purchase a popular product simultaneously. While either factor can lead to a big payday for a star, both factors together make for a superstar payday.

It's possible for Lady Gaga to earn a very large amount of money from a recording session, Keller observed. Customers around the world can each purchase copies of a song. "The possibility for talented persons to command both very large markets and very large incomes is apparent."

The journalist noted that these observations apply both to singers and to superstar financiers active in business and banking. "Do hedge fund managers deserve their paycheques? Do i-bankers?" asked Keller. "In a moral sense, surely not. They planted no crops, educated no children, built no homes, and saved no lives. Then again, neither did Lady Gaga." Keller has no illusions about the morality of banking or of artistic work. As long as the music charts are tracking songs to the top of the pops, "there will be chart-topping bankers," Keller said. "Ye have the poor always with you, said Jesus. And the superstar rich, said Rosen."[16]

TOP 100

In May 2011, *Forbes* business magazine put Lady Gaga at the top of their Celebrity 100 list, above even Oprah Winfrey. It wasn't income alone that put Gaga in the number one position among celebrities. The income from her Monster Ball tour put Gaga's earnings at an estimated $90 million from May 1, 2010, to May 1, 2011.[17] That's less than a third of what Oprah earned from her syndicated show and spin-offs for the stars Dr. Phil, Rachel Ray, and Dr. Oz. The editors of *Forbes* don't deduct management, agent, and attorney fees from income when comparing celebrities for this list. They also try to assess the most powerful people in the business of entertainment by considering how these actors, athletes, models, and singers "rose to the top by garnering influence."[18]

The deciding factor for the assessment by *Forbes* was Gaga's mastery of social media. "Gaga is there . . . because of her 32 million Facebook fans and 10 million Twitter followers—aka Little Monsters—who helped move 1 million digital downloads of her recent single 'Born This Way' in only five days," wrote Dorothy Pomerantz. "They're also happy to buy the MAC makeup, Monster headphones and Virgin Mobile phones she features in her videos."[19]

"Sometimes it pays to be weird. The Queen Monster grossed $170 million on 137 shows in 22 countries over the past 12 months and has sold an estimated 15 million albums worldwide," noted another writer for *Forbes*. "No surprise that advertisers want a piece: endorsement deals include Polaroid, Virgin Mobile, Monster Cable, Viva Glam and PlentyOfFish.com. A Russian billionaire reportedly paid $1 million to appear in her 'Alejandro' video."[20] *Forbes* also noticed that when "Born This Way" was released in May, the song became the fastest-selling song in iTunes history.

CELL PHONE WORRY

There have been rumors that cell phone use may increase the risk of brain cancer. Some of the rumors are based on medical studies. It seems that the rumors have frightened Lady Gaga.

It's almost impossible for a celebrity not to use a cell phone several times a day. This celebrity in particular makes regular use of a cell phone for phone calls, text messages, and regular messages updating her Twitter status.

"[M]ounting evidence of the possible adverse effects of cell-phone radiation in Europe and in Israel has spurred some state legislatures in the United States to take precautionary action," observed journalist Robert Sullivan. He noted that a proposed bill in California legislation would require that cell-phone manufacturers display, as clearly as the price and other features, the radiation emitted by a phone. "In Maine this past spring [2010], a legislator went even further, introducing a bill to require cell-phone manufacturers to put a safety warning in the packaging, similar to the one on cigarette packs, stating that the radiation emitted by the phone has been linked to cancer."[21]

How is Gaga coping with the fear of developing a brain tumor? For one thing, she doesn't dial the phone herself, according to some news articles.[22] One of her entourage keys in the numbers for her. Then the associate turns on the phone's loudspeaker function and holds the phone near Gaga's head, but not too close.

It's quite easy to listen and speak on a cell phone this way, and there are other alternatives as well, for people worried about radiation from phones. Headsets that plug into a cell phone are a good alternative.

HAUNTED

For a modern woman with practical goals and beliefs, Lady Gaga has a few superstitions and spiritual beliefs. She claims to have seen a ghost in London's O2 theatre while there on tour. There are reports that Gaga has had recurring nightmares of a phantom and a blonde girl in bondage wearing the shoes that Gaga wore to the Grammy awards ceremony. Since then, it's been reported that she "has spent thousands of dollars on ghostbusters and splashed out $47,000 on state-of-the-art Electro Magnetic Field meters to detect spirits."[23]

While on tour in Ireland, a member of her crew told the *Daily Star* newspaper that Gaga had been telling the crew for months that she was haunted on her world tour by a male spirit called Ryan. "She's pretty terrified by this spirit, but more than anything he's annoying her as he won't leave her alone. He hasn't been doing anything too violent or scary but she's freaked out by his presence. She's a very spiritual person and in tune with the spiritual world but this is a step too far, even for her."[24]

"She contacted a spirit medium and organized a séance so she could communicate with him and tell him to go away," said a source quoted in an Australian newspaper. "She gathered all her friends over the weekend in Belfast, Ireland, and held the séance to find out what he wants. She's convinced she picked this up as a bad omen. Although most of her friends were skeptical they agreed to take part. She believes in paranormal activity and won't take any risks when she is on the road. It's important to her to be safe from spirits."[25]

SETTING PRIORITIES

"I don't have the same priorities as other people . . . I just don't. I like doing this all the time," Gaga told a *Rolling Stone* reporter. "It's my passion. When I'm not doing a show, I'm writing a song, or I'm on the phone with Dada yapping about a hemline. The truth is, the psychotic woman that I truly am comes out when I'm not working. When I'm not working, I go crazy."[26]

"Eighteen months into her unrelenting extravagant Monster Ball, Stephanie Joanne Angelina Germanotta, a.k.a. Lady Gaga, opened her show in silhouette, posing like an extraterrestrial runway model with a flaming yellow pageboy for her opening song 'Dancing in the Dark,'" wrote a music reviewer in 2011. The pace of her show seemed like a frenetic attack. "From that point on, it was one theatrical set-piece after another, each one more surprising than the last. Gaga played a keyboard in the boot of a large cartoon green Rolls Royce for 'Just Dance' and when her microphone crashed out, she grabbed a second one and yelled, 'At least I don't lip synch!'"[27]

Gaga revealed something of her thoughts about her personal future in an interview for *Rolling Stone*. "Or the little asides, like how she's terrified of [having] babies 'cos she thinks they might mess with her creativity," said writer Neil Strauss, speaking of that interview. "And I think, I wonder what's going to happen in ten years when she does have a kid, how she's going to feel about that then. Because you definitely see people saying things they're going to have to eat their words over later."[28]

"You know how awesome the post-baby Gaga piano tour will be in a few years, after she has a kid and does a huge arena club tour just on piano and with a band?" speculated a blogger for the *Houston Press*. "Ah screw it, Mama Monster would probably dance three days after the kid popped out. Respect."[29]

BIRTHDAY WISHES

Talk show host Ellen DeGeneres made an on-air phone call to wish Lady Gaga a happy 25th birthday. "I can't believe what she's accomplished," said DeGeneres. "When I was twenty-five, I was performing in a basement for three friends." The audience of the show *Ellen* was crowing with excitement, while Gaga sounded both tired and happy. "Take a day off," advised DeGeneres, but the singer was too busy in the studio to take time off.

"I'm so happy and excited and so grateful," Gaga said to DeGeneres. "I can't begin to tell you how shocked and overjoyed I am that 'Born This Way' was still number one for a sixth week. I *loved* your version," she said. It seems that everyone makes videos of their own versions of Lady Gaga songs and puts them on YouTube.

When asked what she'd like for her birthday, Gaga sighed. "For my birthday, I'd *like* the day off. But that's not going to happen. I'm really excited because all my family and friends are flying out to LA. I'm going to be . . . celebrating with all of them."

DeGeneres had a birthday cake made to send to Gaga's party—a vegan cake, of course. When a stagehand brought the cake out on the set, it looked a little like a hat, decorated with several elements from some of Gaga's costumes. There was a bow, crystals, heavy chain links, a Kermit the Frog head, and a red *point d'esprit* lace crown at the top. Smoke puffed out from some attachment on the back. Since Gaga was on the phone, not in the studio, she couldn't see the cake at that moment. But DeGeneres promised to take a picture of it with her cell phone and tweet it, so Gaga could see the cake right away. "Take a day off," DeGeneres advised again, as their call was ending.

"I don't want any time off," Gaga insisted, her energy renewing. "I'm a beast in her cage, I want to be set free so I can bring all this music to you."[30]

POLAROID PRODUCTS

The Consumer Electronics Show is an annual showcase of new electronic devices. At the 2011 show in Las Vegas, Lady Gaga was present to unveil not one, but three new products. A year earlier, Polaroid had named Gaga as the corporation's new creative director. The result was three products that generated a lot of attention.

Most of the attention was focused on the GL20 Camera Glasses. The wearer can take digital pictures with the glasses, and display the

Lady Gaga describes the new Polaroid GL30 instant digital camera during the Consumer Electronics Show, January 6, 2011, in Las Vegas. Lady Gaga is Polaroid's creative director. (AP Photo/Julie Jacobson)

pictures on the lenses. The 1.5-inch (about 3.8 cm) lenses show what was in the field of view for the wearer. The consumer product is based on a pair of glasses worn by Gaga in the video for her song "Telephone."

The second product "will revolutionize how we see photos,"[31] said a statement by Gaga. It's the GL10 Instant Mobile Printer, a small printer for photographs taken on a cell phone. The third item she presented was the GL30 Instant Digital Camera. This digital camera has an option allowing for a photo to be printed out at once, as the classic Polaroid camera used to do.

THE WRITE STUFF

Being appointed a Fashion+Art columnist is a turn in a new creative direction for Gaga. While writing was an important part of her classes in high school and at Tisch, that was years ago. Most of the writing she has done since her time as a student has been songwriting and promotional statements.

It didn't take long for her to write a Twitter update about becoming a magazine writer. "Just turned in my first memorandum as a columnist to my editor at V *Magazine!* How fabulous. Feel like the punk piss-off Carrie Bradshaw."[32] The response from her Twitter followers was positive. But then, so was the response to her August 16, 2011, tweet that said merely "F**K THURSDAY." When a person has 12 million Twitter followers, it's not hard to get 20,000 comments in response to almost any note.

"Art is a lie. And every day I kill to make it true," Gaga wrote in her column for V *Magazine*. "It is my destiny to exist halfway between reality and fantasy at all times . . . I am a show with no intermission . . . Maybe I am not escaping. Maybe I am just being. Being myself. The arrival at this revelation revises my previous escapist philosophies, as my entire being, thus far, as wholly artist and wholly human, has been propelled by the idea that I must effortlessly vacillate between two worlds: out of the real and into the surreal. Out of the ordinary, into the extraordinary."[33]

The ongoing work of writing a regular column will be a new effort. It will also be one more challenge for this creative person. How can she keep up with all her work for Versace and Polaroid and now V *Magazine*, keep making tour appearances, and write any new song material? This column is one more responsibility that she will have to meet on an ongoing basis.

THE LOW POINTS

For Gaga, the hardest thing about her success is being on the road so much. One of the things she has to be on guard for is a recurring depression. She doesn't know what causes these sad feelings, but it seems likely that jet lag and lack of sleep are factors.

"I have a chronic sadness that recurs. The lowest point was in Australia in May," she said in an interview in November 2009. "I was overwhelmingly sad, and I don't know why, because I had all these things to be happy about. I went to the studio and played for hours, and I wrote what is going to be the greatest record of my career, a beautiful song about my father. I remember watching the mascara tears flood the ivories and I thought, 'It's OK to be sad.' I've been trained to love my darkness."[34] The song that came out of that session eventually became "Speechless"—one with a different tone than her usual dance numbers.

While most of Gaga's songs and performances are praised by her many fans, the response from reviewers and critics is not all positive for all her work. "When historians look back on the rise and fall of Lady Gaga, they may pin the beginning of her descent to the day she morphed into a motorbike and made it her album cover," wrote a journalist in the United Kingdom. "The fashion-forward singer has unveiled the artwork for her third LP—and it looks more like a cheap Photoshop job than the most anticipated album of the year."[35]

Rising to the peaks of pop stardom takes hard work, and there isn't always a crowd cheering. "And finally when I got there, I discovered what was at the top," Lionel Richie commented about his own workaholic efforts to reach the top. "You know what was there? Nothing. Not one thing. What was at the top was all the experiences you had to get there."[36]

CAREER PATH FOR THE FUTURE

At this point in Lady Gaga's career, it is powerfully obvious that she is no one-hit wonder. It remains to be seen whether the arc of her career will be more like that of Cyndi Lauper, Madonna, or Cher. It's already clear that Gaga's career path is not that of Amy Winehouse.

In 2011, at 27, Winehouse had been suffering from alcohol and substance abuse for some time when her sudden death came as little or no surprise to her fans, the music industry, and even her family. It can't have escaped Gaga's notice that someone that she was mistaken for at Lollapalooza just a few years ago has now passed away. "Amy changed pop music forever," said the status post Gaga updated on Twitter and Facebook on July 24, 2011. "I remember knowing there was hope, and feeling not alone because of her. She lived jazz, she lived the blues."

There are many singing stars who died at 27, from Janis Joplin and Jimi Hendrix to Kurt Cobain. A superstition has sprung up, claiming that the members of the Forever 27 club, including bluesman Robert Johnson, Brian Jones of the Rolling Stones, and Jim Morrison of The Doors, were subject to some mystic or astrological effect. "The number of musicians who died at 27 is truly remarkable by any standard," wrote Charles R. Cross, a biographer for Cobain and Hendrix. He pointed out that though people die at all ages, "there is a statistical spike for musicians who die at 27."[37] These early deaths may be due to leading a very active lifestyle with access to alcohol and other substances of abuse.

A few months before Winehouse's untimely passing, Gaga's active lifestyle was bringing her access to her fans and the future instead of substances of abuse. One of the more memorable moments in the Monster Ball tour was Lady Gaga's performance to a sold-out house at Canada Place in Toronto. A fan's amateur video taken with a cell phone was played on national news reports on the CBC. When little Maria Aragon was brought onstage to sing "Born This Way," Gaga could be seen with tears in her eyes, watching the little girl with an expression of hope and affection. Most of all, what her face showed was recognition. It was clear to the viewer that in Maria, Gaga saw herself at that age, dressed up and singing, as little Stefani imagined her future.

The attention Gaga gave Maria, and the chance to perform, is a positive sign for the future. "The tearful star called her 'the future,' but Aragon was more than that," wrote reviewer Rupert Everett-Green. "She was the unscarred second draft of the come-from-nowhere success story at the center of Gaga's personal mythology."[38] As a performer Gaga is maturing. No longer is she the self-focused teenage Stefani who didn't let her little sister show what she, too, was doing on the piano.

As the Monster Ball tour rolled on through 2011, reviewers no longer considered Gaga a newcomer. Instead, she was characterized as "Lurid, bitter, swaggering, maternal—and oddly real."[39] Whatever else comes in the meteoric career of Lady Gaga, clearly she is on the right track.

NOTES

1. Thomson, Graeme. "Lady Gaga: The Future of Pop." *The Observer*. Posted November 29, 2009. Retrieved April 20, 2011. http://www.guardian.co.uk/music/2009/nov/29/lady-gaga-interview.

2. Tunstall, Scott. "15 Pics of Lady Gaga Dressed Like an Idiot." *Gunaxin Media*. Posted March 2, 2011. Retrieved April 15, 2011. http://media.gunaxin.com/15-pics-of-lady-gaga-dressed-like-an-idiot/83972?utm_source=scribol&utm_medium=referral&utm_campaign=scribol.

3. BTR. "Lady Gaga: I'm So Excited for Adele." *BraziLadyGaga*. Posted June 2, 2011. Retrieved June 7, 2011. http://braziladygaga. blogspot.com/2011/06/lady-gaga-im-so-excited-for-adele.html.

4. Awehali, Brian. "Mongolia's Wilderness Threatened by Mining Boom." *Earth Island Journal/The Guardian*. Posted January 11, 2011. Retrieved April 14, 2011. http://www.guardian.co.uk/environment/2011/jan/11/mongolia-wilderness-mining-boom?INTCMP=SRCH.

5. Van Meter, Jonathan. "Oprah Goes Gaga." *Vogue*. July 2010, p. 120.

6. Lady Gaga. "Lady Gaga's Oprah Performance." *LadyGaga.com*. Posted May 5, 2011. Retrieved May 8, 2011. http://www.ladygaga.com/news/default.aspx?nid=35402.

7. Everett-Green, Rupert. "Lurid, Bitter, Swaggering, Maternal—and Oddly Real." Globe Arts. *The Globe and Mail*. March 5, 2011, p. R2.

8. Cable, Simon. "Well It Was Bound to Happen . . . Lady Gaga Takes a Tumble Thanks to Her Ridiculous Choice of Footwear." *The Daily Mail Online*. Posted June 24, 2010. Retrieved March 4, 2011. http://www.dailymail.co.uk/tvshowbiz/article-1288980/Lady-Gaga-takes-tumble-thanks-ridiculous-choice-footwear.html.

9. "Lady Gaga Tells All: Rolling Stone's New Issue." *Rolling Stone*. Posted June 21, 2010. Retrieved April 15, 2011. http://www.rollingstone.com/music/news/lady-gaga-tells-all-rolling-stones-new-issue-20100621.

10. Lady Gaga. *Twitter*. Posted March 27, 2011. Retrieved April 10, 2011. http://twitter.com/ladygaga.

11. Alexiou, Joseph. "The Weird Al Yankovic/Lady Gaga Parody Dispute Has Now Been Resolved." *Business Insider*. Posted April 21, 2011. Retrieved April 21, 2011. http://www.businessinsider.com/lady-gaga-weird-al-yankovic-coolio-born-this-way-blocked-2011-4. Page no longer available.

12. Reid, Shaheem. "Mix Tape Mondays." *MTV*. Posted November 9, 2006. Retrieved April 20, 2011. http://www.mtv.com/bands/m/mixtape_monday/091106/.

13. TMZ staff. "Lady Gaga—I Didn't Reject Weird Al Yankovic." *TMZ*. Posted April 20, 2011. Retrieved April 21, 2011. http://www.tmz.com/2011/04/20/weird-al-yankovic-lady-gaga-rejected-born-this-way-parody-perform-this-way/.

14. Yankovic, Al. "Gaga Update!" *Al's Blog*. Posted April 20, 2011. Retrieved April 21, 2011. http://alyankovic.wordpress.com/.

15. Billboard. "Weird Al Goes Digital with T.I. Cover." *Billboard*. Posted October 6, 2008. Retrieved April 20, 2011. http://www.billboard.com/bbcom/news/article_display.jsp?vnu_content_id=1003870753.

16. Keller, Tony. "What Lady Gaga and Hedge Fund Managers Have in Common." *Globe and Mail*. Posted January 26, 2011. Retrieved February 21, 2011. http://www.theglobeandmail.com/report-on-business/rob-magazine/what-lady-gaga-and-hedge-fund-managers-have-in-common/article1879307/.

17. Pomerantz, Dorothy. "Lady Gaga Tops Celebrity 100 List." *Forbes*. Posted May 18, 2011. Retrieved May 18, 2011. http://www.forbes.com/2011/05/16/lady-gaga-tops-celebrity-100–11.html. Page no longer available.

18. Ibid.

19. Ibid.

20. "Lady Gaga" *Forbes*. Posted May 18, 2011. Retrieved May 18, 2011. http://www.forbes.com/profile/lady-gaga.

21. Sullivan, Robert. "Wake-Up Call." *Vogue*. July 2010, p. 130.

22. "Lady Gaga Scared of Using Mobile Phone." *Real Bollywood*. Posted August 31, 2010. Retrieved April 9, 2011. http://www.realbollywood.com/news/2010/08/lady-gaga-scared-mobile-phone.html.

23. "Lady Gaga Holds a Séance to Get Rid of Ghost." *Herald Sun*. Posted November 4, 2010. Retrieved April 2, 2011. http://www.heraldsun.com.au/entertainment/confidential/lady-gaga-holds-seance-to-get-rid-of-annoying-ghost/story-e6frf96o-1225947708797.

24. Brown, Jessica, and Sonja Stephen. "Lady Gaga: I'm Going to Give Up the Ghost!" *Daily Star*. Posted November 3, 2010. Retrieved April 5, 2011. http://www.dailystar.co.uk/playlist/view/161244/Lady-GaGa-I-m-going-to-give-up-the-ghost-/.

25. "Lady Gaga Holds a Séance to Get Rid of Ghost," *Herald Sun*.

26. Hiatt, Brian. "Lady Gaga: New York Doll." *Rolling Stone*. Posted June 11, 2009. Retrieved April 15, 2011. http://www.rollingstone.com/music/news/lady-gaga-new-york-doll-20090611.

27. Armstrong, Denis. "Concert Review: Lady Gaga Scotiabank Place, Ottawa—March 7, 2011." *Jam*. Posted March 8, 2011. Retrieved March 13, 2011. http://jam.canoe.ca/Music/Artists/L/Lady_GaGa/ConcertReviews/2011/03/08/17532381.html.

28. Conner, Shawn. "Interview with Neil Strauss." *Guttersnipe*. Retrieved May 5, 2011. http://www.guttersnipenews.com/features/neil-strauss/.

29. Hlavaty, Craig. "Friday Night: Lady Gaga at Toyota Center." *Houston Press Blogs*. Posted April 11, 2011. Retrieved April 18, 2011. http://blogs.houstonpress.com/rocks/2011/04/lady_gaga_toyota_center.php.

30. Lady Gaga, and Ellen DeGeneris. *Ellen*. Posted March 28, 2011. Retrieved March 28, 2011. http://ellen.warnerbros.com/2011/03/ellens_birthday_call_to_lady_gaga_0328.php.

31. Greene, Andy. "Lady Gaga Unveils Polaroid Sunglasses at CES." *Rolling Stone*. Posted January 7, 2011. Retrieved April 15, 2011. http://www.rollingstone.com/music/news/lady-gaga-unveils-polaroid-sunglasses-at-ces-20110107.

32. Lady Gaga. *Twitter*. Posted April 5, 2011. Retrieved April 10, 2011. http://twitter.com/ladygaga.

33. Lady Gaga. "From the Desk of Lady Gaga." *V Magazine*. Posted July 2011. Retrieved August 10, 2011. http://www.vmagazine.com/2011/07/from-the-desk-of-lady-gaga-2/.

34. Thomson, "Lady Gaga."

35. Michaels, Sean. "Lady Gaga's Born This Way Artwork Provokes Fan Backlash." *The Guardian*. Posted April 18, 2011. Retrieved April 20, 2011. http://www.guardian.co.uk/music/2011/apr/18/lady-gaga-born-this-way-artwork.

36. Empire, Kitty. "Everyone Loves You When You're Dead (and Other Things I Learned from Famous People) by Neil Strauss—Review." *The Observer*. Posted May 15, 2011. Retrieved May 16, 2011. http://www.guardian.co.uk/books/2011/may/15/everyone-loves-you-when-youre-dead-review.

37. Cross, Charles R. "P-I's Writer in Residence Charles R. Cross Explores the Darker Side of 'Only the Good Die Young.'" *Seattle Post-Intelligencer*. Posted February 23, 2007. Retrieved August 2, 2011. http://www.seattlepi.com/default/article/P-I-s-Writer-in-Residence-Charles-R-Cross-1229072.php.

38. Everett-Green, "Lurid, Bitter, Swaggering, Maternal—and Oddly Real," p. R2.

39. Ibid.

Appendix:
RECORDINGS, VIDEOS, AND TOURS

RECORDINGS

Studio Albums	Release Date	Label
The Fame	August 19, 2008	Streamline, Kon Live, Cherrytree, Interscope
Born This Way	May 23, 2011	Streamline, Kon Live, Interscope

Compilation Albums	Release Date	Label
The Remix	March 3, 2010	Streamline, Kon Live, Cherrytree, Interscope
The Singles	December 8, 2010	Streamline, Kon Live, Cherrytree, Interscope

EPs	Release Date	Label
The Cherrytree Sessions	February 3, 2009	Streamline, Kon Live, Cherrytree, Interscope
Hitmixes	August 25, 2009	Streamline, Kon Live, Cherrytree, Interscope

The Fame Monster	November 18, 2009	Streamline, Kon Live, Cherrytree, Interscope

VIDEOS

Video Albums

Year	Title	Label
2010	*The Fame Monster: Video EP*	Streamline, Kon Live, Cherrytree, Interscope
2010	*One Sequin at a Time*	Echo Bridge Home Entertainment

Music Videos

Year	Title	Director
2008	"Just Dance" (featuring Colby O'Donis)	Melina Matsoukas
2008	"Beautiful, Dirty, Rich"	Melina Matsoukas
2008	"Poker Face"	Ray Kay
2009	"Eh, Eh (Nothing Else I Can Say)"	Joseph Kahn
2009	"Love Game"	Joseph Kahn
2009	"Chillin" (Wale featuring Lady Gaga)	Chris Robinson
2009	"Paparazzi"	Jonas Åkerlund
2009	"Bad Romance"	Francis Lawrence
2009	"Video Phone" (extended remix)	Hype Williams (Beyoncé featuring Lady Gaga)
2010	"Telephone" (featuring Beyoncé)	Jonas Åkerlund
2010	"Alejandro"	Steven Klein
2011	"Born This Way"	Nick Knight
2011	"Judas"	Lady Gaga and Laurieann Gibson
2011	"The Edge of Glory"	Haus of Gaga
2011	"Yoü and I"	Laurieann Gibson

Tours

2005	Stefani Live
2006	Lady Gaga and the Starlight Revue
2006	New York Street Revival and Trash Dance
2007	Lady Gaga Revue
2008	Just Dance Promo tour
2008	New Kids on the Block: Live Tour
2009	Doll Domination tour
2009	The Fame Ball
2009	Take That Presents: The Circus Live
2009	The Fame Kills—cancelled
2009	The Monster Ball
2010–11	The Monster Ball 2.0
2011	The Born This Way Ball

BIBLIOGRAPHY

Callahan, Maureen. *Poker Face: The Rise and Rise of Lady Gaga*. New York: Hyperion/HarperCollins, 2010.

Cooke, C.W., Dan Glasl, and Adam Ellis. *Fame: Lady Gaga Vol. 2*. Vancouver, WA: Bluewater Productions, 2011.

Edwards, Posy. *Lady Gaga: Me & You*. London, UK: Orion Books, 2010.

Glamourpuss: The Lady Gaga Story. New Malden, Surrey UK: Sexy Intellectual, 2010.

The Gloss. http://thegloss.com/.

Goodman, Lizzy. *Lady Gaga: Critical Mass Fashion*. New York: St. Martin's Press. 2010.

Herbert, Emily. *Lady Gaga Behind the Fame*. New York: Overlook Press, 2010.

"Lady Gaga." *Facebook*. http://www.facebook.com/ladygaga.

Lady Gaga. *LadyGaga.com*. http://www.ladygaga.com/.

"Lady Gaga." *MySpace*. http://www.myspace.com/ladygaga.

"Lady Gaga." *Twitter*. http://twitter.com/ladygaga.

"Lady Gaga Official's YouTube Channel." YouTube. http://www.youtube.com/ladygaga.

"Lady Gaga VEVO's Channel" VEVO YouTube. http://www.youtube
.com/ladygagavevo.

MTV. http://www.mtv.com.

Parvis, Sarah. *Lady Gaga*. Kansas City, MO: Downtown Bookworks/
Andrews McMeel Publishing, LLC, 2010.

Rafter, Dan, and Tess Fowler. *Fame: Lady Gaga*. Vancouver, WA: Bluewater Productions, 2010.

Rolling Stone. http://www.rollingstone.com/.

INDEX

About the Author

PAULA JOHANSON has worked as a writer and editor for 21 years. Her nonfiction books on science, health, and literature include *World Poetry: Signs of Life* and *Fish: From the Catch to Your Table—The Truth about the Food Supply*. Her novel *Tower in the Crooked Wood* is available in print and as an ebook. She was shortlisted twice for the Prix Aurora Award for Canadian Science Fiction Writing, while raising gifted twins on an organic-method small farm. An accredited teacher, she has edited curriculum educational materials for the Alberta Distance Learning Centre and eTraffic Solutions. Johanson plays folk guitar on an acoustic Gibson and carries noise-reducing earplugs so that loud concerts won't damage her fading hearing.